The Life of God in the Soul of Man

by
Henry Scougal

~~~~~~~~~~~~~~~~~~~~~~~~~~~~~~

to which is added

Rules and Instructions for a Holy Life

by
Robert Leighton

CHRISTIAN HERITAGE

Introduction © J I Packer

ISBN 1-85792-105-4

10 9 8 7 6 5 4 3 2 1

Published in 1996,
reprinted in 2001, 2002 and 2005
in the
Christian Heritage Imprint
by
Christian Focus Publications Ltd.
Geanies House, Fearn, Ross-shire,
IV20 1TW, Scotland, Great Britain.

www.christianfocus.com

Cover design by Owen Daily

Printed and bound by
Nørhaven Paperback A/S, Denmark

Contents

~~~~~~

Introduction

~~~~~~~~~~~~~~~~~~~~~~~~~~~~~~~~~~~~~~

'I never knew what true religion was till God sent me this excellent treatise,' wrote George Whitefield.

When a man of Whitefield's stature applauds a book in such terms, it is our wisdom to sit up and take notice. For who was Whitefield? The 'Grand Itinerant', as his contemporaries called him, was, more than anyone else, the trail-blazing pioneer and personal embodiment of the eighteenth-century revival of vital Christianity in the West, the revival that shaped English-speaking society on both sides of the Atlantic for over a hundred years and that fathered the evangelical missionary movement which for the past two centuries has been taking the gospel literally round the world.

That epoch-making revival threw up many outstanding leaders, but head and shoulders above the rest were four giants, landmark figures not just for their own lifetime but for all later ages too: John Wesley, supreme as organizer, educator, pastoral leader, publicist and apologist; Charles Wesley, his younger brother, sublimest poet of Christian experience; Jonathan Edwards, America's greatest theologian; and with them, indeed in one sense ahead of them all, Whitefield, who for a generation till his death in 1770 was acknowledged as the focal figure of the entire movement. First to preach the transforming message of the new birth, first to take it into the open air and declare the world his parish, first to publish journals celebrating God's work in and through him, and first to set up societies for the nurturing of those who came to faith under his ministry, Whitefield proclaimed Christ tirelessly throughout Britain and colonial America, drawing huge crowds, winning thousands of souls, impacting myriads more, and gaining celebrity status of a kind matched only by Billy Graham and John Paul II today. Wesley's influence as a renewer of popular religion is sometimes credited with saving England from an upheaval like the French revolution; if there is substance in such reasoning, Whitefield should receive greater credit, for his ministry ranged wider and his pulpit power was greater. We live at a time when uncertainty as to what constitutes true religion is more widespread, perhaps, than at any time since Christianity was born; we shall do well to recognize that the little old book that cleared Whitefield's mind on this basic matter might have something to say to us too.

Henry Scougal's exposition of 'true religion' (his phrase, echoed by Whitefield, meaning genuine Christianity) was from one standpoint the seed out of which the English side of the revival first sprouted; for the book was favourite reading in Oxford's Holy Club, where the Wesleys and Whitefield first came together. For half a century religious societies, as they were called, had been set up in various places to supplement the parish church's Sunday ministry by midweek gatherings for prayer, discussion, and the reading of works of devotion ('good books'). The society lampooned as the Holy Club was run by John Wesley in his capacity as an ordained priest and Fellow of Lincoln College. It was distinctive only for being in Oxford, where such a thing had not, it seems, been seen before, and for the ascetic intensity with which its dozen or so members pursued the goal of true religion. Whitefield, a tall, good-looking, well-spoken freshman from Gloucester, a servitor at Pembroke College – one, that is, who performed menial duties to finance his education – admired the Holy Club from afar, and wanted to join. Charles Wesley, himself a member, took a liking to Whitefield and gave him Scougal, which he eagerly devoured. An agonizing quest, evidently Scougal-sparked, for the life of God in his own soul then led to the dawning of an assured certainty that through the grace of Jesus Christ he was 'ransomed, healed, restored, forgiven' and truly born again.

I once heard a Christian testify, 'I knew I was converted when religion stopped being a duty and became a delight,' and that is something Whitefield could have said, for that was precisely what he felt. Once ordained, he preached the new birth as the door of entry into true religion as Scougal described it, and the English revival began. Without Scougal it might not have happened.

What precisely was it that Whitefield learned from Scougal? In a word, it was the inwardness and supernaturalness of biblical godliness. Not that Scougal's testimony here was in any way unique. During the century that followed the Reformation conflicts, English Puritans like Perkins, Owen and Baxter, Anglicans of the 'holy living' school like Jeremy Taylor, Lutheran pietists like Johannes Arndt, and Roman Catholic teachers like Ignatius Loyala, Francis de Sales, Teresa of Avila and John of the Cross, had all centred attention on the realities of the Christian's inner life, to such an extent that scholars can nowadays speak of the seventeenth-century devotional revival. In this study the Reformation debates about church, sacraments, justification and authority largely receded into the background; communion with the Father and the Son through the Spirit, lived out in the disciplined practice of patient love and humble obedience, was the common theme, and Scougal, a devoted soul himself, was able to draw on a rich legacy of fairly homogeneous thought about 'the life of God in the soul of man'. This helps to explain the extraordinary authority, maturity, and sureness of touch with which at the age of 26 he was able to analyze the reality of spiritual life. Granted, he was brilliant and precocious (he served as Professor of Philosophy in Aberdeen University for four years, from the age of 19); granted, he was the son of a bishop, and a godly one, and had had every spiritual advantage in his upbringing plus, as it seems, a heart responsive to God from his earliest days; but even so, he could hardly have produced this little classic – for such it is – without the distilled wisdom of the seventeenth century behind him.

'Christians,' declares Scougal, 'know by experience that true religion is a union of the soul with God, a real participation of the divine nature, the very image of God drawn upon the soul, or, in the apostle's phrase, "it is Christ formed within us".' It is 'life', the life of God within, in the sense of being spontaneous energy actively responding to the grace of God set forth in the gospel. Scougal calls it 'an inward, free and self-moving principle ... a new nature instructing and prompting'. Love, purity and humility are the three fundamental virtues in which this life takes form, and all three are blos-

somings of faith. 'Faith (is) ... a kind of sense, or
feeling persuasion of spiritual things; it extends
itself unto all divine truths; but in our lapsed
estate, it hath a peculiar relation to the declarations of God's mercy and reconcilableness to
sinners through a mediator; and therefore ... is
ordinarily termed "faith in Jesus Christ".' The
virtues themselves are to be conceived in a way
that sees acts as the outworking of attitudes
and attitudes as the expression of motives; so
Scougal defines them as follows.

Love, basically, is love of God: 'a delightful
and affectionate sense of the divine perfections,
which makes the soul resign and sacrifice itself
wholly unto him, desiring above all things to
please him, and delighting in nothing so much
as in fellowship and communion with him, and
being ready to do or suffer anything for his sake,
or at his pleasure ... A soul thus possessed with
divine love must needs be enlarged towards
all mankind ... this is ... charity ... under which
all parts of justice, all the duties we owe to our
neighbour, are eminently comprehended; for
he who doth truly love all the world ... so far
from wronging or injuring any person ... will
resent any evil that befalls others, as if it happened to himself.'

Purity is 'a due abstractedness from the body
and mastery over the inferior appetites ... such
a temper and disposition of mind as makes a
man despise and abstain from all pleasures

and delights of sense or fancy which are sinful in themselves, or tend to ... lessen our relish of more divine and intellectual (he means, God-centred and rational) pleasures, which doth also infer a resoluteness to undergo all those hardships he may meet with in the performance of his duty: so that not only chastity and temperance, but also Christian courage and magnamity may come under this head.'

And humility means 'a deep sense of our own meanness, with a hearty and affectionate acknowledgment of our owing all that we are to the divine bounty; which is always accompanied with a profound submission to the will of God, and great deadness to the glory of the world, and the applause of men.'

'These qualities,' says Scougal, 'are the very foundation of heaven laid in the soul,' just as they are the basic elements of genuine Christ-likeness here and now. The rest of his book is a celebration of these qualities, with encouragement to develop habits of repentance and discipline in using the means of grace (thought, prayer, and the Lord's Supper) so as to engender all three ever more radically and robustly in one's personal life.

Scougal never loses sight of the inwardness of true religion, as a state of being that starts in our hearts, nor of the fact that it is a supernatural product, 'having God for its author, and being wrought in the souls of men by the power of the

Holy Spirit'; so we do not find him slipping into
the self-reliant, performance-oriented, surface-
level, ego-focussed, living-by-numbers type of
instruction that is all too common among Christians today. He knows that personal change
will not occur without use of means, just as he
knows that no use of means will change the
heart without God's blessing, and he marks out
the path of change with admirable balance.

One could wish, however, that his exposition had been more explicitly and emphatically
Christ-centred. Like so many seventeenth-century writers, he lets himself assume that his
readers know all about Jesus and need only
to be told about real religion, the life of faith
and faith-full turning Godward as opposed to
the orthodoxism, formalism, emotionalism
and legalism that masquerade as Christianity
while being in truth a denial of it. Had Scougal
elaborated on the Christian's union with Christ,
which the New Testament sees as regeneration
by the Holy Spirit; had he explained incorpo-
ration into the Saviour's risen life, whereby
Jesus's motivating passion to know and love
and serve and please and honour and glorify
the Father is implanted in sinners so that it is
henceforth their own deepest desire too; had he
thus shown, in black and white, that imitating
Jesus's aims and attitudes in serving God and
mankind is for the born-again the most natural,
indeed the only natural, way of living, while

for the unregenerate it is hard to the point of impossible; his little treatise would have been immeasurably stronger. As it is, Scougal's profile of divine life in human souls is much more complete than his answer to the question, how do I get into it? – or, how does it get into me? This is a limitation.

To be sure, there are real strengths in Scougal's account of the means of grace for the changing of the heart, particularly when he directs us to meditation – sustained thought, that is – on the 'vanity and emptiness of worldly enjoyments', the truth of Christianity, and the redeeming love of God as shown in the saving ministry of our Lord Jesus Christ. He is strong too when he urges us to form habits of behaving as if our hearts were changed even though as yet they are not. This is more than 'fake it till you make it'; Scougal is telling us to give God proof that we are serious and sincere in seeking inward renewal, for he knows that evidence of sincerity is something God regularly requires as a condition of answering our prayers. With these emphases, however, should be linked specific directions on looking to and coming to the living Christ himself, believing on him, trusting in him, and waiting for him till we know that we are his and he is ours – the sort of directions that Whitefield himself was later to give during the last half-hour of many thousands of evangelistic messages. Scougal's omission here, which leaves the impression that godliness blossoms in us as a kind of natural growth, is certainly a shortcoming.

It will be appropriate as we close to cite more fully Whitefield's witness to what Scougal gave him. This comes from a sermon preached in the last year of his life, taken down as he spoke and not corrected.

'When I was sixteen years of age, I began to fast twice a week for thirty-six hours together, prayed many times a day, received the sacrament every Lord's day, fasting myself almost to death all the forty days of Lent, during which I made it a point of duty never to go less than three times a day to public worship, besides seven times a day to my private prayers, yet I knew no more that I was to be born again in God, born a new creature in Christ Jesus, than if I were never born at all ...
I must bear testimony to my old friend Mr Charles Wesley; he put a book into my hands, called *The Life of God in the Soul of Man*, whereby God showed me, that I must be born again, or be damned.

I know the place: it may be superstitious, perhaps, but whenever I go to Oxford, I cannot help running to that place where Jesus Christ first revealed himself to me, and gave me the new birth ... How did my heart rise, how did my heart shudder, like a poor man that is afraid to look into his account-books, lest he should find himself a bankrupt; yet shall I burn that book, shall I throw it down, shall I put it by, or shall I search into it? I did, and holding the book in my hand, thus addressed the God of heaven and earth: Lord, if I am not a Christian, if I am not a real one, God, for Jesus Christ's sake, show me what Christianity is, that I may not be damned at last. I read a little further ... O, says the author, they that know anything of religion, know it is a vital union with the Son of God, Christ formed in the heart; O what a ray of divine life did then break in upon my poor soul ... from that moment God has been carrying on his blessed work in my soul: and as I am now fifty-five years of age ... I tell you, my brethren ... I am more and more convinced that this is the truth of God, and without it you never can be saved by Jesus Christ ...'

Thus God used Scougal to awaken the man who himself came later to be known as the Awakener. And all that remains to be said is that some today, who would call themselves Christians if asked, clearly stand in need of a similar awakening: which Scougal, under God, may bring them, if only they will read his smooth late-seventeenth-century rhetoric thoughtfully and let it speak to them. Real Christians will gain from Scougal a healthy reminder that heart-change and character-change thence resulting is what their faith is all about, and the self-deceived will be forced to face the fact that those who have not yet been so changed are not yet Christians at all. Scougal's word to them will thus have been preparation for the humble hearing of the gospel invitation, which many today will fail to hear because they are unaware that they need to hear it, and which Whitefield, near the time when he uttered the testimony quoted above, verbalized as follows:

'Sinners in Zion, baptised heathens, professors but not possessors, formalist, believing unbelievers, talking of Christ, talking of grace, orthodox in your creeds, but heterodox in your lives, turn ye, turn ye, Lord help you to turn to him, turn ye to Jesus Christ, and may God turn you inside out ... may that glorious Father that raised Christ from the dead, raise your dead souls! ... Bless the Lord that Jesus stands with pitying eyes, and outstretched arms, to receive you now. Will you go with the man? Will you accept of Christ? Will you begin to live now? May God say, Amen; may God pass by, not in anger, but in love ... and say to you dead sinners, come forth, live a life of faith on earth, live a life of vision in heaven; even so, Lord Jesus: *Amen.*'

J. I. Packer

to third, and which will is this that the value when he attended to be it is the question and ignited at his right

Preface

~~~~~~~~~~~~~~~~~~~~~~~~~~~~~~~~~~~~~

This age groans under such a surcharge of new books, that, though the many good ones lately published do much balance the great swarms of ill, or at least needless ones; yet all men complain of the unnecessary charge and trouble many new books put them to: the truth of it is, printing is become a trade, and the presses must be kept going, so that, if it were but to shuffle out an ill book, a man may be tempted to keep them at work.

And for books of devotion and piety we have seen so many excellent ones of late in our own language, that perhaps no age or language can show the like: in these the Christian religion is proposed in its own true and natural colours, and rescued from those false representations many are apt to make of it; as if it consisted either in external performances, or in mechanical hearts to the fancy, or in embracing some opinions or interests. 'It is, and can be nothing else, but a design to make us like God, both in the inward temper of our minds, and in our whole deportment and conversation.' For this end did Christ both live and die; this he taught by discourses, and discovered in his life. He died, that he might take away sin, and not only, or chiefly to procure our pardon, which was done by him for a further end, than an universal indemnity being offered through his death, all mankind might be thereby encouraged to enter into a course of holy obedience with all possible advantages, having the hopes of endless happiness, and the fears of eternal miseries before them; having the clearest rule, and the most unblemished example proposed to them; being also sure of constant inward supplies, to support and strengthen their endeavours, and an unerring providence to direct all things that concern them.

Nor are there any precepts in this whole doctrine, whose fitness and true excellency, besides the authority of the Law-giver, has not been fully made good: and the truth of the principles of natural religion, and of the revelation of the counsel of God in Scripture, was never, since miracles ceased, demonstrated with fuller and clearer evidence than in our age; both for stopping the mouths of all daring Hectors, and for silencing the secret doubtings of more inquisitive minds. And though so grave a subject should have been rather prejudiced than adorned by artificial and forced strains of wit and eloquence; yet as our language was never chaster than now, so these subjects have been handled with all the proper decencies of easy wit and good language.

But, after all this, into what a torrent of grief and lamentation must we break out, when we consider the age we live in! for few, do either believe or reflect on those great things: and, as if there were a general conspiracy against God and religion, how does the great part among us break loose from all the ties and bonds of that yoke that is light and easy, and enslave themselves to many base and hurtful lusts and passions? and are not satisfied with being as bad as they can be, but desire that all the world may esteem them such, and glory in their shame; and enhance their guilt by turning factors for hell, studying to corrupt all about them.

This sad prospect must needs deeply affect all that either truly love God, or have a tender compassion for the souls of men; and will certainly set them to their secret mournings and wrestlings with God, to avert the heavy judgments that seem to hang over our heads, and that he may, of his great mercy, turn the hearts of the froward and disobedient to the wisdom of the just.

And, till God arise and bless his Gospel with more of this success, nothing could be such an effectual means for convincing the world of the truth and excellency of our most holy faith, as that those who profess and embrace it, did walk in all the strictness of a most holy, innocent, and exemplary life; keeping the due mean between the affection of moroseness and hypocrisy, and the levities of irreligion and folly. This is the only argument that is wanting to convince the world of the truth of our religion: all people are more wrought on by lively examples set before their eyes than by any discourses or reasonings, how strong and convincing soever: the one is more easily apprehended, and leaves a deeper impression than the other, which does not prevail on us, till by frequent and serious reflections we be satisfied about them; and when we hear any one speak well, we are not assured he thinks as he says, but do often suspect he is showing his wit or eloquence to our cost, that he may persuade us into some opinions that may prove gainful to himself. But when we see a man pursuing a constant course of holiness in the most painful instances, which do most prejudice his visible interests, we have all the reason to believe he is in good earnest persuaded of those truths, which engage him to such a conversation.

After the age of miracles, nothing prevailed so much on the world as the exemplary lives, and the painful martyrdoms of the Christians; which made all sorts of people look with amazement on that doctrine that wrought so powerfully on all ranks, and did raise persons of the meanest educations and dispositions, and of the weaker sex, and tender age, to do and suffer beyond what their greatest heroes and most celebrated philosophers had ever done. And in those days, the apologists for the Christian religion did appeal to the lives of the Christians to prove their doctrine to be holy; concluding, that there could be nothing but good in that doctrine which made all its votaries such. But alas! when we write apologies, we must appeal from the lives of most that pretend to be religious, to the rules and precepts of our most holy faith, and must decline the putting the trial of Christianity upon that issue; and though, thanks be to God, there are beautiful and shining instances of the power of religion among us; yet, alas! there be too few of them, and they lie hid in a vast mixture of others that are naught.

The two great prejudices, the tribes of Libertines and Ruffians, hardened in against religion, are: First, that they do not see those that profess they believe the truths of religion, live like men that do so in good earnest; and I have known them say, that did they believe the great God governed all human affairs, and did know all we do, and would call us to an account for it, and reward or punish accordingly, in an endless and unchangeable state, they could not live as the greater part of Christians do, but would presently renounce all the vanities and follies of this world, and give themselves up wholly to a holy and exact course of life.

Secondly, the other prejudice is, that as for those in whose deportment they find little to blame, yet they have great cause of suspecting there is some hidden design under it, which will break out when there is a fit opportunity for it, and they conclude, that such persons are either secretly as bad as others, only disguising it by a more decent deportment, or that all they do is a force upon themselves for some secret end or other. And if there be some on whom they can fasten neither of these, as it is hardly possible but one that is resolved to possess himself with prejudices will either find or pretend some colours for them, then, at last, they judge such persons are morose or sullen, and that they find, either from the disposition of their body, or their education, as much satisfaction in such their sour gravity, as others do in all their wanton and extravagant follies.

These prejudices, especially the first, must be discussed by real confutations; and the strict conduct of our lives, as well as our grave and solemn devotions, must show, we are over-ruled by a strong belief of the authority of that law which governs out whole actions. Nor will our abstaining from gross immoralities be argument enough, since even decency may prevail so far; though, alas! never so little as now, when fools do so generally mock at the shame and sense of sin, as if that were only the peevishness of a strict and liberal education, but we must abstain from all those things that are below the gravity of a Christian, and which strengthen a corrupt generation in their vices.

What signifies endless gaming, especially when joined with so much avarice and passion as accompany it generally, but that people know not how to dispose of their time, and therefore must play it away idly at best? What shall be said of those constant crowds at plays: 'especially when the stage is so defiled with atheism, and all sorts of immorality', but, that so many persons know not how to fill up so many hours of the day, and therefore this contrivance must serve to waste them, and they must fill their eyes and ears with debauching objects, which will either corrupt their minds, or at least fill their imaginations with very unpleasant and hateful representations? as if there was not a sufficient growth of ill thoughts ready to spring up within us, but this must be cultivated and improved by art.

What are those perpetual visits, in the giving or receiving of which most spend the better half of the time in which they are awake; and how trifling at best, but generally how hurtful the discourses that pass in those visits are, I leave to those who live in them to declare. How much time is spent in vain dressing, not to mention those indecent arts of painting, and other contrivances to corrupt the world, and all, either to feed vanity, or kindle lust? and after all this, many that live in these things desire to be thought good Christians, are constant at church, and frequent at the sacrament.

What wonder then, if our libertines, seeing such things in persons that pass for very religious, and having wit enough to discern that such a deportment does not agree with the belief of an account to be made for all we do, conclude, they do not believe it, otherwise they would not behave themselves as they do. Some failures, now and then, could not justify such an inference; but a habit and course of those things is an argument against the reality of that belief, which I confess I cannot answer.

But, when we have got so far as to escape those things that are blame-worthy, it is far from being all we must aim at, it is not enough not to be ill; we must be good, and express it in all the circumstances which our state of life and circumstances call for. Doing good to all, forgiving injuries, comforting all in trouble, supplying the necessities for the poor; but chiefly, studying to advance the good of all people's souls as much as we can; improving whatever interest we have in any persons to this end, of raising them to a sense of God and another life: the chief motive we offered to this, being the unaffected strictness of our own deportment, which will make all our discourses have the greater weight and force in them.

And for the other prejudices, it is true, there is no fence or security against jealousy, yet we ought carefully to avoid every thing that may be an occasion of it; as all secret converse with suspected persons, the doing any thing, that without sin we may forbear, which is singular, or may bring a disesteem on others, or make us be observed, or talked of; and, in a word, to shun all forced gestures, or modes of speech, and every thing that is not native and genuine: for, let men think what they will, nothing that is constrained can ever become so natural, but it will appear loathsome and affected to others; which must needs afford matter of jealousy and disesteem, especially to prying and critical observers.

Were there many who did live thus, the atheists would be more convinced, at least more ashamed, and out of countenance, than the most learned writings or laboured sermons will ever make them; especially if a spirit of universal love and goodness did appear more among Christians, and those factions and animosities were laid aside, which both weaken the inward vitals of holiness, and expose them to the scorn of their adversaries, and make them an easy prey to every aggressor.

There is scarce a more unaccountable thing to be imagined, than to see a company of men professing a religion, one great and main precept whereof is mutual love, forbearance, gentleness of spirit, and compassion to all sorts of persons, and agreeing in all the essential parts of its doctrine, and differing only in some less material and more disputable things, yet maintaining those differences with zeal so disproportioned to the value of them, and prosecuting all that disagree from them with all possible violence; or if they want means to use outward force, with all bitterness of spirit. They must needs astonish every impartial beholder, and raise great prejudices against such person's religion, as made up of contradictions; professing love, but breaking out in all the acts of hatred.

But the deep sense I have of these things has carried me too far; my design in this Preface being only to introduce the following discourse, which was written by a pious and learned country man of mine, for the private use of a noble friend of his, without the least design of making it more public. Others seeing it, were much taken both with the excellent purposes it contained, and the great clearness and pleasantness of the style, the natural method, and the shortness of it, and desired it might be made a more public good; and knowing some interest I had with the Author, it was referred to me, whether it should lie in a private closet, or be let go abroad. I was not long in suspense, having read it over; and the rather, knowing so well as I do, that the Author has written out nothing here but what he himself did well feel and know; and therefore it being a transcript of those divine impressions that are upon his own heart, I hope the native and unforced genuineness of it, will both more delight and edify the reader. I know these things have often been discoursed with great advantages both of reason, wit, and eloquence; but the more witnesses that concur in sealing these divine truths with their testimonies, the more evidence is thereby given.

It was upon this account that the Author having seen a letter written by a friend of his to a person of great honour, but far greater worth, of the *Rise and Progress of a Spiritual Life*, wherein, as there were many things which he had not touched, so in those things of which they both discourse, the harmony was so great, that he believed they would mutually strengthen one another, was earnest with his friend that both might go abroad together and the other pressing him to let his discourse be published, he would not yield to it, until he granted the same consent for his.

And so the reader has both, the one after the other; which he is desired to peruse with some degrees of the same seriousness in which they were both penned, and then it is presumed he will not repent him of his pains.

G. Burnet

A brief notice of the life of the
Rev Henry Scougal MA
Sometime Professor of Philosophy and
Divinity in the University of Aberdeen

~~~~~~~~~~~~~~~~~~~~~~~~~~~~~~~~~~~~~

The Rev Henry Scougal was the second son of the Rev Patrick Scougal and Margaret Wemys. His father was Bishop of Aberdeen for more than twenty years after the Restoration. His eldest sister, Catherine, married Alexander Scrogie, Bishop of Argyle; and Jane, the younger, was the wife of Patrick Sibbald, a minister of Aberdeen. Henry Scougal, the subject of this notice, was born in June 1650. He was the worthy son of a worthy sire. His father is commended by Bishop Burnet for his purity, humility and gentleness. 'He was,' says the Bishop, 'the common father of his whole diocese, and esteemed no less by the Dissenters than by the Conformists. A set of men grew up under his labours that carry still on them clear characters of his spirit and temper.'

The memoirs which have been prefixed to the 'Works of Henry Scougal' seem to have been compiled from the sermon preached at his

funeral, by the Rev George Gairden, DD, from
the text, 'For me to live is Christ, and to die is
gain'. This sermon was first published from an
authentic manuscript by the Rev Mr Cockburn,
minister of St Paul's, Aberdeen. It is one of the
most elaborate eulogies we have ever read. The
preacher seemed to labour with emotion, and
to regard himself as the representative of Scotland's grief over a national calamity. But for its
great length, we should have included it in this
volume; as it is, we must content ourselves with
cutting from it and other sources such incidents
in the life of our author as will satisfy the very
natural curiosity of those who are edified by
his writings.

His father devoted him from his infancy to the
service of God in the sanctuary, and was very
diligent in training him in the way in which he
wished him to go. Accordingly, the son, who was
of a most sweet and serene temper, employed
those leisure-hours, which are generally spent
by children in play, in reading, meditation and
prayer.

Like Timothy, he knew the Holy Scriptures
from his childhood, and could give an account
of the scope of the sermons which he heard. He
preferred the conversation of serious persons
to the foolish stories in which children so much
delight. His progress in human learning was in
proportion to his other attainments. He acquired
a singular elegance in the Latin language, and

a commendable proficiency in Greek, Hebrew and other oriental tongues, being well versed in history and in the mathematics. Such was his quickness of apprehension, that from overhearing an occasional discourse of some students, he learned the nature of a syllogism, and could form one upon any subject.

He was now qualified for the higher branches of learning, and at fifteen years of age, he entered the University of Aberdeen. His course in college was as brilliant as his early promise. He not only soon ran through the learning then in fashion, but anticipated the coming age in his philosophical researches.

His life, at the same time, was a model of religious propriety, and his devotional spirit took the form of ingenious and elegant moral essays, and pious meditations. Such was his reputation among his fellow-students, that he was chosen to preside at their meetings; and his 'discourses were so grave and becoming that they thought they savoured of the wisdom of a Senator'.

So soon as he came out of the University, he was thought worthy to be a master, where he had been so lately a scholar. After a brief trial, he was made Professor of Philosophy in his nineteenth year. Young as he was, he proved himself equal to the duties of his high trust. He was the first to introduce into Scotland, and perhaps into the nation, that philosophy which has been since taught with such brilliant success in the Scottish universities, and been received with such general favour by men of science everywhere.

He was careful to train his students in the principles of morality, and to guard them against the subtleties of infidelity. Humility and learning were so beautifully blended in him as to make it evident that philosophy and religion were not enemies to one another, but that the sober use of reason makes us more capable of the graces of the Gospel. He assembled the students every Sunday evening, and 'had pious discourses' with them, representing the folly and wickedness of vice, and the beauties and excellencies of virtue. He also sought private interviews with them, studying to reform what was amiss, and to call out and cherish every sign of grace.

He filled this chair with honour to himself and blessings to the University for four years. But God designed him for more immediate service to his Church, to which he had been devoted from the womb; and therefore, by the counsels of his father and other reverend friends, he took orders, and entered upon the charge of the parish of Auchterless, a small village, about twenty miles from Aberdeen. During his short ministry in this parish, he gave singular proofs of his fitness for, and zeal in his new vocation.

Some idea may be formed of his views of the fearful responsibilities of this high office from the following extracts from a sermon which he preached before the synod of Aberdeen upon the 'Importance and Difficulty of the Ministerial Function':

'Like people, like priests, is a proverb generally true. *Causa sunt ruina populi, mali sacerdotes.* But if the negligence of a minister doth hazard the souls of others, it doth certainly ruin his own, which made St Chrysostom say: *Equidem ex ecclesiae ministris non arbitror multos servari,* or words so terrible that I tremble to put them into English. And yet, if a man should speak fire, and blood, and smoke, if flames should come out of his mouth instead of words, if he had a voice like thunder, and an eye like lightning, he could not sufficiently represent the dreadful account which an unfaithful pastor shall make...

'Again, preaching is an exercise of which many are ambitious, and none more so than those that are the least qualified for it; but it is not so easy a matter to perform this task aright. To stand in the presence of God, and speak to his people in his name, with that seriousness, gravity and simplicity, that zeal and concern which the business requires; to accommodate ourselves to the capacity of the common people, without disgusting the more knowing ones; to awaken drowsy souls, without terrifying tender consciences; to carry home the charge of sin, without the appearance of personal reflection; in a word, to approve ourselves unto God as workmen that need not be ashamed, rightly dividing the word of truth.

'You see, sirs, to what a dreadful and important charge you aspire. Consider, I beseech you, what great pains are necessary to fit you for it. It is not a knowledge of controversy, or the gift of eloquence; much less, a strong voice and bold confidence, that will prepare you for it. Your *greatest work lies within*, in purifying yourselves, and learning that wisdom which is necessary to win souls. Begin, I pray you, and preach to your passions, and try what good you can do to your *friends* and *neighbours*. Be not forward in rushing into public; it is better to be *drawn* than to run.

'Again, we are not to entertain our people with subtle questions, and metaphysical niceties, etc. Let us study to acquaint them with the tenor of the *Gospel-covenant*, and *what they must do to be saved*; and teach them their duties to God and men. But it is not enough to *speak these things*, to *tell* men what their duty is; we must endeavour to stir them up by the most powerful and effectual persuasions. The judgment being informed, we must move the affections and this is the *proper use of our preaching*. "The people that commonly sit under the pulpit (as the excellent Herbert observes) are usually as hard and dead as the seats they sit on, and need a mountain of fire to kindle them." The best way is to preach the things first to ourselves, and then frequently to recollect in whose presence we are, and whose business we are doing.'

He looked upon it as a most useful help in composing sermons to make the Sunday's sermon the subject of meditation and prayer for the foregoing week, that it might sink deep into the spirits and affect the heart, while it would make one more capable of teaching others. He also thought it a fit expedient in the meditations to desire purely the glory of God and the good of men's souls; and to have this always in our eye; and in our preaching to make frequent recollections of the divine presence, and shout ejaculations to heaven, thereby to preserve us in that humble and serious temper that becomes the ambassadors of Christ in the presence of God.

He had a deep sense of the value of true eloquence, and thought that there were two essential defects in our best kinds of speaking. The first was, that in meditating discourses, ministers rather considered the issues of reason and the nature of things than the temper and circumstances of the persons to whom they were going to speak, and what kind of words and reasonings would make the best impression upon their minds; and, therefore, he said, words let fly at random so seldom hit the mark. The other was that our hearts were so seldom endued with those dispositions we would work in others by our words; and, therefore, it was no wonder all we said made so little impression on them. His own practice was (according to the testimony of his contemporaries) a beautiful example of his theory.

His discourses are said to have been so full of thought, his style so plain, his manner of utterance and gesture so sweet, and so expressive of his concern for souls, as quite charmed men's spirits. 'And all was so full of light and heart,' says Dr Gairden, 'that I may say in the words of our Saviour, "Did not our hearts burn within us, while he opened to us the Scriptures?"'

In public worship, and especially in celebrating the Holy Communion, his whole soul seemed to be swallowed up in the contemplation of Jesus Christ.

During his pastoral charge, the hardships he endured were the common talk of all who knew him; his coarse fare and hard lodging, the extreme coldness of the season, and his comfortless shelter from it, excited the compassion of others, but never clouded the serenity and cheerfulness of his spirit.

He had a high estimate of the value of catechising, and was very diligent in the practice of it. He also attached great importance to the firm, yet meek administration of discipline, saying, 'that it was an edged tool, and they had need be no fools who meddled with it'. He thought that ministers should not miss a day in which they do not treat *personally* and in *private*

with some of their people about the affairs of
their souls.

His advices about the personal character and
manners of ministers were unusually judicious
in one so young. Ministers, he said, should be-
ware of the least imputation of covetousness,
for they would be more blamed for claiming
their own than others for encroaching on their
neighbours. He was, accordingly, very liberal
in all his dealings, laying aside upon principle
the first fruits of all his revenues for the service
of God. He seemed literally to take no thought
what he ate or drank, and wherewithal he was
clothed. He thought it strange to see a Christian,
who should be an example of temperance, taking voluptuous pleasure in meats, making them
the subject of their table-talk, and declaring
that they loved such and such dishes with all
their hearts, as if they owned their bellies for
their God.

He quotes with approbation the saying of
Jerome to Nepotian. '*Facile contemnitur cleri-
cus si ad prandium invitatus saepius veniat.*'
After remaining in this charge about a year, and
having enjoyed the love of his flock almost to
adoration, he was summoned by the unanimous
voice of the clergy of the diocese of Aberdeen
to the Divinity-chair of the University. He was
eminently fitted by his genius, learning and
character for this place. His care of the students
under his charge was more strict than under his

former professorship. His attention to the duties of his office was equally assiduous.

Of all the branches of science which he taught, the Pastoral Care and Casuistical Divinity were those in which he most delighted; the latter with the view of preparing Protestant divines to refute the subtleties of the Jesuits.

To his pupils he was ever affectionate and kind, ever ready to assist them with books and instructions. He was faithful in teaching them at stated seasons the nature and requisites of the Holy Office, and admonishing them of the duties which it laid upon them.

Just as his friends were confidently hoping that his labours, with God's blessing, would put 'another face on the Church', he became the victim of consumption, which put an end to his life on the 13th June 1678, before he had completed his twenty-eighth year. The time of his sickness was as cheerfully spent in *suffering* the will of God as the time of his health in *doing* it. 'He used not the least harsh expression, either to those who waited upon him, or concerning the present Providence.' He was wrapt in admiration of God's goodness to him, and perfectly submissive to his will.

The end of his life was no less 'Christ's' than the beginning and whole course of it. Thus meekly did he pass his sickness, and resign his spirit, amid the lamentations of the entire community. Every man who knew or heard of him (says a contemporary) claims a share in our grief, and bewails a particular loss. His father remembers a most dutiful son; relations cry out for the loss of their dearest kinsman; the learned bemoan the want of a great divine and promoter of true knowledge; the youth lament the deprivation of a most pious, wise, and affectionate guide; the poor grieve for the loss of a father; the devout miss their director and pattern; the Church one of her purest lights; the clergy their example and honour; the people the blessings of his life and doctrine; the whole nation the want of its ornament and a great promoter of all graces and virtue; yea, and other sects confess that a few like him would heal all our schisms. He was buried in Kings' College Church, Old-Aberdeen, with the following inscription upon his tombstone:

Memoriae Sacrum
Henricus Scougal
Reverendi in Christo Patris Patricii Episcopi
Aberdanensis Filius
Philosophiae in hac Academia Regia
Per Quadriennium Todidemque Annis
Ibidem Theologiae Professor
Ecclesiae in Auchterless uno anno interstitae
Pastor
Multa in tam Brevissimo Curriculo Didicit,
Peaestitit,
Docuit, Coeli Avidus et Coelo Maturus
Obiit Anno Dominus MDCLXXVIII
Aetatis suae XXVIII
Et Hic Exuvias Mortalitatis Posuit.

The above memoir is compiled from Dr Gairden's sermon; from Scougal's own sermons, of which nine have been published; from sketches in former editions of our author's works, and from the Encyclopedia.

Part 1

The Occasion of this Discourse

∿∿∿∿∿∿∿∿∿∿∿∿∿∿∿∿∿∿∿∿∿∿∿∿∿

My Dear Friend:

This designation doth give you a title to all the endeavours whereby I can serve your interests; and your pious inclinations do so happily conspire with my duty, that I shall not need to step out of my road to gratify you; but I may at once perform an office of friendship, and discharge an exercise of my function, since the advancing of virtue and holiness, which I hope you make your greatest study, is the peculiar business of my employment.

This therefore is the most proper instance wherein I can vent my affection, and express my gratitude toward you, and I shall not any longer delay the performance of the promise I made you to this purpose: for though I know you are provided with better helps of this nature than any I can offer you, nor are you like to meet with any thing here which you knew not before; yet I am hopeful, that what cometh from one whom you are pleased to honour with

41

your friendship, and which is more particularly designed for your use, will be kindly accepted by you; and God's providence, perhaps, may so direct my thoughts that something or other may prove useful to you. Nor shall I doubt your pardon, if for moulding my discourse into the better frame, I lay a low foundation, beginning with the nature and properties of religion, and all along give such way to my thoughts, in the prosecution of the subject, as may bring me to say many things which were not necessary, did I only consider to whom I am writing.

Mistakes about religion

I cannot speak of religion, but I must lament, that among so many pretenders to it, so few understand what it means; some placing it in the understanding, in orthodox notions and opinions; and all the account they can give of their religion is, that they are of this or the other persuasion, and have joined themselves to one of those many sects whereinto Christendom is most unhappily divided.

Others place it in the outward man, in a constant course of external duties, and a model of performances; if they live peaceably with their neighbours, keep a temperate diet, observe the returns of worship, frequent the church, or their closet, and sometimes extend their hands to the relief of the poor, they think they have sufficiently acquitted themselves.

Others again put all religion in the affections, in rapturous heats and ecstatic devotion; and all they aim at is, to pray with passion, to think of heaven with pleasure, and to be affected with those kind and melting expressions wherewith they court their Saviour, till they persuade themselves that they are mightily in love with him, and from thence assume a great confidence of their salvation, which they esteem the chief of Christian graces.

Thus are these things which have any resemblance of piety, and at the best are but means of obtaining it, or particular exercises of it, frequently mistaken for the whole of religion. Nay, sometimes wickedness and vice pretend to that name. I speak not now of those gross impieties wherewith the heathens were wont to worship their gods; there are but too many Christians who would consecrate their vices, and hallow their corrupt affections, whose rugged humour, and sullen pride, must pass for Christian severity; whose fierce wrath, and bitter rage against their enemies, must be called holy zeal; whose petulancy towards their superiors, or rebellion against their governors, must have the name of Christian courage and resolution.

What religion is
But certainly religion is quite another thing, and they who are acquainted with it will entertain far different thoughts, and disdain all those

shadows and false imitations of it. They know by experience that true religion is a union of the soul with God, a real participation of the Divine nature, the very image of God drawn upon the soul, or, in the apostle's phrase, 'it is Christ formed within us'. Briefly, I know not how the nature of religion can be more fully expressed, than by calling it a Divine life: and under these terms I shall discourse of it, showing first how it is called a life, and then how it is termed Divine.

Its permanency and stability

I choose to express it by the name of life; first, because of its permanency and stability. Religion is not a sudden start, or passion of the mind, nor though it should rise to the height of a rapture, and seem to transport a man to extraordinary performances.

There are few but have convictions of the necessity of doing something for the salvation of their souls, which may push them forward some steps with a great deal of seeming haste, but anon they flag and give over; they were in a hot mood, but now they are cooled; they did shoot forth fresh and high, but are quickly withered; because they had no root in themselves. These sudden fits may be compared to the violent and convulsive motions of bodies newly beheaded, caused by the agitations of the animal spirits, after the soul is departed, which however violent and impetuous, can be of no long continuance; whereas the motions of holy souls are constant and regular, proceeding from a permanent and lively principle.

It is true, this Divine life continueth not always in that same strength and vigour, but many times suffers sad decays, and holy men find greater difficulty in resisting temptations, and less alacrity in the performance of their duties; yet it is not quite extinguished, nor are they abandoned to the power of those corrupt affections, which sway and over-rule the rest of the world.

Its freedom and unconstrainedness

Again, religion may be designed by the name of life; because it is an inward, free and self-moving principle; and those who have made progress in it, are not acted only by external motives, driven merely by threatenings, nor bribed by promises, nor constrained by laws; but are powerfully inclined to that which is good, and delight in the performance of it.

The love which a pious man bears to God and goodness, is not so much by virtue of a command enjoining him so to do, as by a new nature instructing and prompting him to it; nor doth he pay his devotions as an unavoidable tribute, only to appease the Divine justice, or quiet his clamorous conscience; but those religious exercises are the proper emanations of the Divine life, the natural employments of the new-born soul. He prays, and gives thanks, and repents, not only because these things are commanded, but rather because he is sensible of his wants, and of the Divine goodness, and of the folly and misery of a sinful life; his charity is not forced, nor his alms extorted from him, his love makes him willing to give; and though there were no outward obligation, his 'heart would devise liberal things'; injustice or intemperance, and all other vices, are as contrary to his temper and constitution, as the basest actions are to the most generous spirit, and impudence and scurrility to those who are naturally modest: so that I may well say with St John, 'Whosoever is born of God doth not commit sin: for his seed remaineth in him, and he cannot sin because he is born of God' (1 John 3:9). Though holy and religious persons do much eye the law of God, and have a great regard unto it, yet it is not so much the sanction of the law, as its reasonableness, and purity, and goodness, which do prevail with them. They account it excellent and desirable in itself, and that in keeping of it there is great reward; and that Divine love wherewith they are acted makes them become a law unto themselves.

Quis legem det amantibus?
Major est amor lex ipse sibi.

Who shall prescribe a law to those who love?
Love's a more powerful law which doth them move.

In a word, what our blessed Saviour said of himself, is in some measure applicable to his followers, 'that it is their meat and drink to do their Father's will' (John 4:34). And as the natural appetite is carried out toward food, though we should not reflect on the necessity of it for the preservation of our lives; so are they carried with a natural and unforced propensity toward that which is good and commendable. It is true, external motives are many times of great use to excite and stir up this inward principle, especially in its infancy and weakness, when it is often so languid, that the man himself can scarce discern it, hardly being able to move one step forward, but when he is pushed by his hopes, or his fears, by the pressure of an affliction, or the sense of a mercy, by the authority of the law, or the persuasion of others.

Now if such a person be conscientious and uniform in his obedience, and earnestly groaning under the sense of his dullness, and is desirous to perform his duties with more spirit and vigour; these are the first motions of the Divine life, which though it be faint and weak, will surely be cherished by the influences of heaven, and grow unto greater maturity. But he who is utterly destitute of this inward principle, and doth not aspire unto it, but contents himself with those performances whereunto he is prompted by education or custom, by the fear of hell, or carnal notions of heaven, can no more be accounted a religious person, than a puppet can be called a man.

This forced and artificial religion is commonly heavy and languid, like the motion of a weight forced upward: it is cold and spiritless, like the uneasy compliance of a wife married against her will, who carries it dutifully toward the husband whom she doth not love, out of some sense of virtue or honour. Hence also this religion is scant and niggardly, especially in those duties which do greatest violence to men's carnal inclinations, and those slavish spirits will be sure to do no more than is absolutely required; it is a law that compels them, and they will be loth to go beyond what it stints them to; nay, they will ever be putting such glosses on it, as may leave themselves the greatest liberty: whereas the spirit of true religion is frank and liberal, far from such peevish and narrow reckoning; and he who hath given himself entirely unto God, will never think he doth too much for him.

Religion a Divine principle

By this time I hope it doth appear, that religion is with a great deal of reason termed a life, or vital principle, and that it is very necessary to distinguish betwixt it and that obedience which is constrained, and depends on external causes.

I come next to give an account why I designed it by the name of Divine life; and so it may be

called, not only in regard of its fountain and
original, having God for its author, and being
wrought in the souls of men by the power of
his Holy Spirit; but also in regard of its nature,
religion being a resemblance of the Divine perfections, the image of the Almighty shining in
the soul of man: nay, it is a real participation
of his nature, it is a beam of the eternal light,
a drop of that infinite ocean of goodness; and
they who are endued with it, may be said to
have 'God dwelling in their souls', and 'Christ
formed within them'.

What the natural life is

Before I descend to a more particular consideration of that Divine life wherein true religion
doth consist, it will perhaps be fit to speak a little
of that natural or animal life which prevails in
those who are strangers to the other; and by this
I understand nothing else but our inclination
and propensity toward those things which are
pleasing and acceptable to nature; or self-love
issuing forth and spreading itself into as many
branches as men have several appetites and
inclinations: the root and foundation of the
animal life I reckon to be sense, taking it largely,
as it is opposed unto faith, and importeth our
perception and sensation of things that are
either grateful or troublesome to us.

Now these animal affections, considered in
themselves, and as they are implanted in us by

nature, are not vicious or blamable; nay, they are instances of the wisdom of the Creator, furnishing his creatures with such appetites as tend to the preservation and welfare of their lives. These are instead of a law unto the brute beasts, whereby they are directed toward the ends for which they were made; but man being made for higher purposes, and to be guided by more excellent laws, becomes guilty and criminal when he is so far transported by the inclinations of his lower life as to violate his duty, or neglect the higher and more noble designs of our creation. Our natural affections are not wholly to be extirpated and destroyed, but only to be moderated and over-ruled by a superior and more excellent principle. In a word, the difference betwixt a religious and a wicked man is, that in the one, Divine life bears sway, in the other, the animal life doth prevail.

The different tendencies of the natural life
But it is strange to observe unto what different courses this natural principle will sometimes carry those who are wholly guided by it, according to the divers circumstances that concur with it to determine them: and then not considering this doth frequently occasion very dangerous mistakes, making men think well of themselves by reason of that seeming difference which is betwixt them and others, whereas, perhaps, their actions do all the while flow from one and the same original.

If we consider the natural temper and constitution of men's souls, we shall find some to be airy, frolicksome, and light, which makes their behaviour extravagant and ridiculous; whereas others are naturally serious and severe, and their whole carriage composed into such gravity as gains them a great deal of reverence and esteem.

Some are of a humorous, rugged, and morose temper, and can neither be pleased themselves, nor endure that others should be so; but all are not born with such sour and unhappy dispositions; for some persons have a certain sweetness and benignity rooted in their natures, and they find the greatest pleasure in the endearments of society, and the mutual complacency of friends, and covet nothing more than to have everybody obliged to them; and it is well that Nature hath provided this complexional tenderness to supply the defect of true charity in the world, and to incline men to do something for one another's welfare.

Again, in regard of education, some have never been taught to follow any other rules than those of pleasure or advantage; but others are so inured to observe the strictest rules of decency and honour, and in some instances of virtue, that they are hardly capable of doing any thing which they have been accustomed to look upon as base and unworthy.

In fine, it is no small difference in the deportment of mere natural men that doth arise from
the strength or weakness of their wit or judgment, and from their care or negligence in using them. Intemperance and lust, injustice and
oppression, and all those other impieties which
abound in the world, and render it so miserable,
are the issues of self-love, the effect of the animal
life, when it is neither overpowered by religion,
nor governed by natural reason; but if it once
take hold of reason, and get judgment and wit
to be of its party, it will many times disdain the
grosser sort of vices, and spring up unto fair
imitations of virtue and goodness.

If a man have but so much reason as to consider the prejudice which intemperance and
inordinate lust do bring unto his health, his
fortune, and his reputation, self-love may suffice to restrain him; and one may observe the
rules of moral justice, in dealing with others,
as the best way to secure his own interest, and
maintain his credit in the world.

But this is not all; this natural principle, by
the help of reason, may take a higher flight, and
come nigher the instances of piety and religion:
it may incline a man to the diligent study of
Divine truths; for why should not these as well
as other speculations be pleasant and grateful
to curious and inquisitive minds? It may make
men zealous in maintaining and propagating
such opinions as they have espoused, and be

very desirous that others should submit unto their judgment, and approve the choice of religion which themselves have made; it may make them delight to hear and compose excellent discourses about the matters of religion; for eloquence is very pleasant whatever be the subject. Nay, some it may dispose to no small height of sensible devotion.

The glorious things that are spoken of heaven may make even a carnal heart in love with it; the metaphors and similitudes made use of in Scripture, of crowns and sceptres, and rivers of pleasure, etc, will easily affect a man's fancy, and make him wish to be there, though he neither understand nor desire those spiritual pleasures which are described and shadowed forth by them; and when such a person comes to believe that Christ has purchased those glorious things for him, he may feel a kind of tenderness and affection towards so great a benefactor, and imagine that he is mightily enamoured with him, and yet all the while continue a stranger to the holy temper and spirit of the blessed Jesus; and what hand the natural constitution may have in the rapturous devotions of some melancholy persons hath been excellently discovered of late, by several learned and judicious pens.

To conclude, there is nothing proper to make a man's life pleasant, or himself eminent and conspicuous in the world, but this natural principle, assisted by wit and reason, may prompt him to it; and though I do not condemn these things in themselves, yet it concerns us nearly to know and consider their nature, both that we may keep within due bounds, and also that we may learn never to value ourselves on the account of such attainments, nor lay the stress of religion upon our natural appetites or performances.

Wherein the Divine life doth consist

It is now time to return to the consideration of that Divine life whereof I was discoursing before, that 'life which is hid with Christ in God', and therefore hath no glorious show or appearance in the world, and to the natural man will seem a mean and insipid notion. As the animal life consisteth in that narrow and confined love which is terminated in a man's self, and in his propension toward those things that are pleasing to nature; so the Divine life stands in a universal and unbounded affection, and in the mastery over our natural inclinations, that they may never be able to betray us to those things which we know to be blamable.

The root of the Divine life is faith; the chief branches are love to God, charity to man, purity and humility; for, as an excellent person hath well observed, however these names be common and vulgar, and make no extraordinary sound, yet do they carry such a mighty sense, that the tongue of man or angel can pronounce nothing more weighty or excellent.

Faith hath the same place in the Divine life, which sense hath in the natural, being indeed nothing else but a kind of sense, or feeling persuasion of spiritual things; it extends itself unto all Divine truths; but in our lapsed estate, it hath a peculiar relation to the declarations of God's mercy and reconcilableness to sinners through a mediator; and therefore, receiving its denomination from that principal object, is ordinarily termed 'faith in Jesus Christ'.

The love of God is a delightful and affectionate sense of the Divine perfections, which makes the soul resign and sacrifice itself wholly unto him, desiring above all things to please him, and delighting in nothing so much as in fellowship and communion with him, and being ready to do or suffer any thing for his sake, or at his pleasure. Though this affection may have its first rise from the favours and mercies of God toward ourselves, yet doth it, in its growth and progress, transcend such particular considerations, and ground itself on his infinite goodness, manifested in all the works of creation and providence.

A soul thus possessed with Divine love must need be enlarged toward all mankind, in a sincere and unbounded affection, because of the relation they have to God, being his creatures, and having something of his image stamped upon them; and this is that charity I named as the second branch of religion, and under which all the parts of justice, all the duties we owe to our neighbour are eminently comprehended; for he who doth truly love all the world will be nearly concerned in the interest of every one; and so far from wronging or injuring any person, that he will resent any evil that befalls others, as if it happened to himself.

By purity, I understand a due abstractedness from the body and mastery over the inferior appetites; or such a temper and disposition of mind as make a man despise and abstain from all pleasures and delights of sense or fancy which are sinful in themselves, or tend to extinguish or lessen our relish of more Divine and intellectual pleasures, which doth also infer a resoluteness to undergo all those hardships he may meet with in the performance of his duty; so that not only chastity and temperance, but also Christian courage and magnanimity may come under this head.

Humility imports a deep sense of our own meanness, with a hearty and affectionate acknowledgement of our owing all that we are to the Divine bounty; which is always accompanied with a profound submission to the will of God, and great deadness toward the glory of the world, and applause of men.

These are the highest perfections that either men or angels are capable of; the very foundation of heaven laid in the soul; and he who hath attained them need not desire to pry into the hidden rolls of God's decrees, or search the volumes of heaven to know what is determined about his everlasting condition; but he may find a copy of God's thoughts concerning him written in his own breast. His love to God may give him assurance of God's favour to him; and those beginnings of happiness which he feels in the conformity of the powers of his soul to the nature of God, and compliance with his will, are a sure pledge that his felicity shall be perfected and continued to all eternity; and it is not without reason that one said: 'I had rather see the real impressions of a godlike nature upon my own soul, than have a vision from heaven, or angel sent to tell me that my name were enrolled in the book of life'.

Religion better understood by actions than words
When we have said all that we can, the secret mysteries of a new nature and divine life can never be sufficiently expressed; language and words can not reach them; nor can they be truly understood but by those souls that are enkindled within, and awakened unto the sense and relish of spiritual things: 'There is a spirit in man, and the inspiration of the Almighty giveth this understanding'.

The power and life of religion may be better expressed in actions than in words, because actions are more lively things, and do better represent the inward principle whence they proceed: and therefore we may take the best measure of those gracious endowments from the deportment of those in whom they reside; especially as they are perfectly exemplified in the holy life of our blessed Saviour, a main part of whose business in this world was, to teach, by his practice, what he did require of others, and to make his own conversation an exact resemblance of those unparalleled rules which he prescribed: so that, if ever true goodness was visible to mortal eyes, it was then, when his presence did beautify and illustrate this lower world.

Divine love exemplified in our Saviour

That sincere and devout affection wherewith his blessed soul did constantly burn toward his heavenly Father, did express itself in an entire resignation to his will; it was this was his very meat, to do the will and finish the work of him that sent him.

His diligence in doing God's will

This was the exercise of his childhood, and the constant employment of his riper age; he spared no travel or pains while he was about his Father's business, but took such infinite content and satisfaction in the performance of it, that, when being faint and weary with his journey, he rested himself on Jacob's well, and entreated water of the Samaritan woman, the success of his conference with her, and the accession that was made to the kingdom of God, filled his mind with such delight, as seemed to have redounded to his very body, refreshing his spirits, and making him forget the thirst whereof he complained before, and refuse the meat which he had sent his disciples to buy. Nor was he less patient and submissive in suffering the will of God, than diligent in doing of it.

His patience in bearing it
He endured the sharpest of all afflictions and extremest miseries that ever were inflicted on any mortal, without a repining thought or discontented word; for though he was far from a stupid insensibility, or a fantastic or stoical obstinacy, and had as quick a sense of pain as other men, and the deepest apprehension of what he was to suffer in his soul, as his 'bloody sweat, and the sore amazement and sorrow' which he professed, do abundantly declare, yet did he entirely submit to that severe dispensation of Providence, and willingly acquiesced in it.

And he prayed to God, that 'if it were possible', or, as one of the Evangelists hath it, 'if he were willing, that cup might be removed'; yet he gently added, 'nevertheless, not my will but thine be done'. Of what strange importance are the expressions (John 12:27), where he first acknowledgeth the anguish of his spirit, 'Now is my soul troubled', which would seem to produce a kind of demur, 'and what shall I say'; and then he goes to deprecate his suffering, 'Father, save me from this hour'; which he had no sooner uttered, but he doth, as it were, on second thoughts, recall it in these words, 'but for this cause came I into the world'; and concludes, 'Father, glorify thy name'.

Now we must not look on this as any levity, or blamable weakness in the blessed Jesus; he knew all along what he was to suffer, and did most resolutely undergo it; but it shows us the unconceivable weight and pressure that he was to bear, which being so afflicting and contrary to nature, he could not think of without terror; yet considering the will of God, and the glory which was to redound to him from thence, he was not only content, but desirous to suffer it.

His constant devotion

Another instance of his love to God was, his delight in conversing with him by prayer, which made him frequently retire himself from the world, and with the greatest devotion and pleasure spend whole nights in that heavenly exercise, though he had no sins to confess, and but few secular interests to pray for; which, alas! are almost the only things that are wont to drive us to our devotions: nay, we may say his whole life was a kind of prayer; a constant course of communion with God: if the sacrifice was not always offering, yet was the fire still kept alive:

nor was ever the blessed Jesus surprised with that dullness, or tepidity of spirit, which we must many times wrestle with, before we can be fit for the exercise of devotion.

His charity to men

In the second place, I should speak of his love and charity toward all men; but he who would express it must transcribe the history of the Gospel, and comment upon it: for scarce any thing is recorded to have been done or spoken by him which was not designed for the good and advantage of some one or other. All his miraculous works were instances of his goodness as well as his power; and they benefited those on whom they were wrought, as well as they amazed the beholders. His charity was not confined to his kindred or relations; nor was all his kindness swallowed up in the endearments of that peculiar friendship which he carried toward the beloved disciple; but every one was his friend who obeyed his holy commands (John 15:14); and 'whosoever did the will of his Father', the same was to him as 'his brother, and sister, and mother'.

Never was any unwelcome to him who came with an honest intention, nor did he deny any request which tended to the good of those that asked it; so that what was spoken of that Roman Emperor, whom for his goodness they called 'the darling of mankind', was really performed

by him, that never any departed from him
with a heavy countenance, except that youth
(Mark 10), who was sorry to hear that the
kingdom of heaven stood at so high a rate, and
that he could not save his soul and his money
too. And certainly it troubled our Saviour, to
see, that when a price was in his hand to get
wisdom, yet he had no heart to it: the ingenuity
[ingenuousness] that appeared in his first address, had already procured some kindness for
him; for it is said, 'and Jesus, beholding him,
loved him': but must he, for his sake, cut out
a new way to heaven, and alter the nature of
things, which make it impossible that a covet-
ous man should be happy?

And what shall I speak of his meekness? Who
could encounter the monstrous ingratitude and
dissimulation of that miscreant who betrayed
him in no harsher terms than these, 'Judas, be-
trayest thou the Son of Man with a kiss?' What
further evidence could we desire of his fervent
and unbounded charity, than that he willingly laid
down his life even for his most bitter enemies;
and mingling his prayer with his blood, besought
the Father that his death might not be laid to their
charge, but might become the means of eternal
life to those very persons who procured it?

His purity
The third branch of the divine life is purity,
which, as I said, consists in a neglect of worldly

enjoyments and accommodations, in a resolute enduring of all such troubles as we meet with in the doing of our duty.

Now surely, if ever any person was wholly dead to all the pleasures of the natural life, it was the blessed Jesus, who seldom tasted them when they came in his way; but never stepped out of his road to seek them. Though he allowed others the comforts of wedlock, and honoured marriage with his presence; yet he chose the severity of a virgin life, and never knew the nuptial bed: and though, at the same time, he supplied the want of wine with a miracle, yet he would not work one for the relief of his own hunger in the wilderness; so gracious and divine was the temper of his soul, in allowing to others such lawful gratifications as himself thought good to abstain from, and supplying not only their more extreme and pressing necessities, but also their smaller and less considerable wants.

We many times hear of our Saviour's sighs, groans, and tears; but never that he laughed, and but once that he rejoiced in spirit; so that through his whole life, he did exactly answer that character given of him by the prophet of old, that he was 'a man of sorrows, and acquainted with grief.'

Nor were the troubles and disaccommodations of his life other than matters of choice; for never did there any appear, on the stage of the world, with greater advantages to have raised himself to the highest secular felicity. He who could bring together such a prodigious number of fishes into his disciples' net, and, at another time, receive that tribute from a fish which he was to pay to the temple, might easily have made himself the richest person in the world; nay, without any money, he could have maintained an army powerful enough to have justled Caesar out of his throne, having oftener than once fed several thousands with a few loaves and small fishes; but, to shew how small esteem he had of all the enjoyments in the world, he chose to live in so poor and mean a condition, that 'though the foxes had holes, and the birds of the air had nests, yet he, who was Lord and heir of all things, had not whereon to lay his head'.

He did not frequent the courts of princes, nor affect the acquaintance or converse of great ones; but being reputed the son of a carpenter, he had fishermen and such other poor people for his companions, and lived at such a rate as suited with the meanness of that condition.

His humility

And thus I am brought unawares to speak of his humility, the last branch of the divine life; wherein he was a most eminent pattern to us, that we might 'learn of him to be meek and lowly in heart'.

I shall not now speak of that infinite conde-
scension of the eternal Son of God, in taking
our nature upon him; but only reflect on our
Saviour's lowly and humble deportment while
he was in the world.

He had none of those sins and imperfections
which may justly humble the best of men; but
he was so entirely swallowed up with a deep
sense of the infinite perfections of God, that he
appeared as nothing in his own eyes; I mean, so
far as he was a creature. He considered those
eminent perfections, which shined in his blessed
soul, not as his own, but the gifts of God; and
therefore assumed nothing to himself or them,
but, with the profoundest humility, renounced
all pretences to them.

Hence did he refuse that ordinary compella-
tion of good master, when addressed to his human nature by one who, it seems, was ignorant
of his divinity: 'Why callest thou me good, there
is none good but God only'; as if he had said, the
goodness of any creature, and such only thou
takest me to be, is not worthy to be named or
taken notice of; 'tis God alone who is originally
and essentially good.

He never made use of his miraculous power
for vanity or ostentation; he would not gratify
the curiosity of the Jews with a sign from heaven,
some prodigious appearance in the air; nor
would he follow the advice of his countrymen
and kindred, who would have had all his great

works performed in the eyes of the world, for gaining him the greater fame; but when his charity had prompted him to the relief of the miserable, his humility made him many times enjoin the concealment of the miracle; and when the glory of God, and the design for which he came into the world, required the publication of them, he ascribed the honour of all to his Father, telling them, 'that of himself he was able to do nothing'.

I cannot insist on all the instances of humility in his deportment towards men; his withdrawing himself when they would have made him a king; his subjection not only to his blessed mother, but to her husband, during his younger years, and his submission to all the indignities and affronts which his rude and malicious enemies did put upon him. The history of his holy life, recorded by those who conversed with him, is full of such passages as these; and indeed the serious and attentive study of it is the best way to get right measures of humility, and all the other parts of religion, which I have been endeavouring to describe.

But now, that I may lessen your trouble of reading a long letter, by making some pauses in it; let me here subjoin a prayer, that might be proper when one who had formerly entertained some false notions of religion begins to discover what it is.

A Prayer

Infinite and eternal Majesty, author and fountain of being and blessedness, how little do we poor sinful creatures know of thee, or the way to serve and please thee! We talk of religion, and pretend unto it; but, alas! how few are there that know and consider what it means! How easily do we mistake the affections of our nature, and issues of self-love, for those divine graces which alone can render us acceptable in thy sight!

It may justly grieve me to consider, that I should have wandered so long, and contented myself so often with vain shadows, and false images of piety and religion; yet I cannot but acknowledge, and adore thy goodness, who hast been pleased, in some measure, to open mine eyes, and let me see what it is at which I ought to aim. I rejoice to consider what mighty improvements my nature is capable of, and what a divine temper of spirit doth shine in those whom thou art pleased to choose, and causest to approach unto thee.

Blessed be thine infinite mercy, who sentest thine own Son to dwell among men, and instruct them by his example, as well as his laws, giving them a perfect pattern of what they ought to be. Oh! that the holy life of the blessed Jesus may be always in my thoughts, and before mine eyes, till I receive a deep sense and impression of those excellent graces that shined so eminently in him; and let me never cease my endeavours, till that new and divine nature prevail in my soul, and Christ be formed within me.

Part 2

The Excellency and Advantage of Religion

~~~~~~~~~~~~~~~~~~~~~~~~~~~~~~~~~~~~~

And now, my dear friend, having discovered the nature of true religion, before I proceed any further, it will not perhaps, be unfit to fix our meditations a little on the excellency and advantages of it, that we may be excited to the more vigorous and diligent prosecution of those methods whereby we may attain so great a felicity. But, alas! what words shall we find to express that inward satisfaction, those hidden pleasures which can never rightly be understood, but by those holy souls who feel them? 'A stranger intermeddleth not with their joys' (Proverbs 14:10).

Holiness is the right temper, the vigorous and healthful constitution of the soul: its faculties had formerly been enfeebled and disordered, so that they could not exercise their natural functions; it had wearied itself with endless tossings and rollings, and was never able to find any rest; now that distemper being removed, it feels itself well, there is due harmony in its faculties, and a sprightly vigour possesseth every part. The understanding can discern what is good, and the will can cleave unto it; the affections are not tied to the motions of sense, and the influence of external objects; but they are stirred by more divine impressions, are touched by a sense of invisible things.

The excellency of divine love

Let us descend, if you please, into a nearer and more particular view of religion, in those several branches of it which were named before: let us consider that love and affection wherewith holy souls are united to God, that we may see what excellency and felicity is involved in it.

Love is that powerful and prevalent passion by which all the faculties and inclinations of the soul are determined, and on which both its perfection and happiness depend. The worth and excellency of a soul is to be measured by the object of its love: he who loveth mean and sordid things doth thereby become base and vile; but a noble and well-placed affection doth advance and improve the spirit unto a conformity with the perfections which it loves.

The images of these do frequently present themselves unto the mind, and by a secret force and energy insinuate into the very constitution of the soul, and mould and fashion it into their own likeness: hence we may see how easily lovers and friends do slide into the imitation of the persons whom they affect; and how, even before they are aware, they begin to resemble them, not only in the more considerable instances of their deportment, but also in their voice and gesture, and that which we call their mien and air; and certainly we should as well transcribe the virtues and inward beauties of the soul, if they were the object and motive of our love.

But now, as all the creatures we converse with have their mixture and alloy, we are always in hazard to be sullied and corrupted by placing our affection on them: passion doth easily blind our eyes, so that we first approve, and then imitate the things that are blamable in them.

The true way to improve and ennoble our souls is, by fixing our love on the divine perfections, that we may have them always before us, and derive an impression of them on ourselves, and 'beholding with open face, as in a glass, the glory of the Lord, we may be changed into the same image, from glory to glory'.

He who, with a generous and holy ambition, hath raised his eyes toward that uncreated beauty and goodness, and fixed his affection there, is quite of another spirit, of a more excellent and heroic temper than the rest of the world, and cannot but infinitely disdain all mean and unworthy things; will not entertain any low or base thoughts which might disparage his high and noble pretensions.

Love is the greatest and most excellent thing we are masters of; and therefore it is folly and baseness to bestow it unworthily; it is, indeed, the only thing we can call our own, other things may be taken from us by violence; but none can ravish our love: if any thing else be counted ours, by giving our love, we give all, so far as we make over our hearts and wills, by which we possess our other enjoyments: it is not possible to refuse him anything to whom, by love, we have given ourselves: nay, since it is the privilege of gifts to receive their value from the mind of the giver, and not to be measured by the event, but by the desire, he who loveth, may, in some sense, be said not only to bestow all that he hath, but all things else which may make the beloved person happy; since he doth heartily wish them, and would really give them, if they were in his power: in which sense it is that one makes bold to say, 'That divine love doth, in a manner, give God unto himself, by the complacency it takes in the happiness and perfection of his nature': but though this may seem too strained an expression, certainly love is the worthiest present we can offer unto God, and it is extremely debased, when we bestow it another way.

When this affection is misplaced, it doth often vent itself in such expressions as point at its genuine and proper object, and insinuate where it ought to be placed. The flattering and blasphemous terms of adoration, wherein men do sometimes express their passion, are the language of that affection which was made and designed for God: as he who is accustomed to speak to some great person, doth perhaps, unawares, accost another with those titles he was wont to give to him: but, certainly, that passion which accounteth its object a Deity, ought to be bestowed on him who really is so; those unlimited submissions, which would debase the soul if directed to any other, will exalt and ennoble it when placed here: those chains and cords of love are infinitely more glorious than liberty itself: this slavery is more noble than all the empires in the world.

The advantages of divine love

Again, as divine love doth advance and elevate the soul; so it is that alone which can make it happy: the highest and most ravishing pleasures, the most solid and substantial delights that human nature is capable of, are those which arise from the endearments of a well-placed and successful affection. That which imbitters love, and makes it ordinarily a very troublesome and hurtful passion, is the placing it on those who have not worth enough to deserve it, or affection and gratitude to requite it, or whose absence may deprive us of the pleasure of their converse, or their miseries occasion our trouble. To all these evils are they exposed whose chief and supreme affection is placed on creatures like themselves; but the love of God delivers us from them all.

The worth of the object

First, I say, love must needs be miserable, and
full of trouble and disquietude, when there is
not worth and excellency enough in the object
to answer the vastness of its capacity: so eager
and violent a passion can not but fret and torment the spirit, when it finds not wherewith to
satisfy its cravings: and, indeed, so large and
unbounded is its nature, that it must be extremely pinched and straitened, when confined
to any creature: nothing below an infinite good
can afford it room to stretch itself, and exert its
vigour and activity. What is a little skin-deep
beauty, or some small degrees of goodness, to
match or satisfy a passion which was made for
God; designed to embrace an infinite God? no
wonder lovers do so hardly suffer any rival, and
do not desire that others should approve their
passion by imitating it: they know the scanti-
ness and narrowness of the good which they
love, that it cannot suffice two, being in effect
too little for one. Hence love, 'which is strong
as death', occasioneth 'jealousy, which is cruel
as the grave'; the coals whereof are coals of fire,
which hath a most violent flame.

But divine love hath no mixture of this gall;
when once the soul is fixed on that supreme and
all-sufficient good, it finds so much perfection
and goodness as doth not only answer and satisfy
its affection, but master and overpower it too: it
finds all its love to be too faint and languid for

such a noble object, and is only sorry that it can command no more. It wisheth for the flames of a seraph, and longs for the time when it shall be wholly melted and dissolved into love: and because it can do so little itself, it desires the assistance of the whole creation, that angels and men would concur with it in the admiration and love of those infinite perfections.

The certainty to be beloved again
Again, love is accompanied with trouble, when it misseth a suitable return of affection: love is the most valuable thing we can bestow, and by giving it, we do, in effect, give all that we have; and therefore it must needs be afflicting to find so great a gift despised, that the present which one hath made of his whole heart can not prevail to obtain any return.

Perfect love is a kind of self-dereliction, a wandering out of ourselves; it is a kind of voluntary death, wherein the lover dies to himself, and all his own interests, not thinking of them, nor caring for them any more, and minding nothing but how he may please and gratify the party whom he loves: thus, he is quite undone, unless he meets with reciprocal affection; he neglects himself, and the other hath no regard to him; but if he be beloved, he is revived, as it were, and liveth in the soul and care of the person whom he loves; and now he begins to mind his own concernments, not so much because they are his, as because the beloved is pleased to own an interest in them: he becomes dear unto himself, because he is so unto the other.

But why should I enlarge on so known a matter? Nothing can be more clear than that the happiness of love depends on the return it meets with; and herein the divine lover hath unspeakably the advantage, having placed his affection on him whose nature is love, whose goodness is as infinite as his being, whose mercy prevented us when we were his enemies, therefore cannot choose but embrace us when we are become his friends. It is utterly impossible that God should deny his love to a soul wholly devoted to him, and which desires nothing so much as to serve and please him; he cannot disdain his own image, nor the heart in which it is engraven: love is all the tribute which we can pay him, and it is the sacrifice which he will not despise.

The presence of the beloved person
Another thing which disturbs the pleasure of love, and renders it a miserable and unquiet passion, is absence and separation from those we love. It is not without a sensible affliction that friends do part, though for some little time; it is sad to be deprived of that society which is so delightful, our life becomes tedious, being spent in an impatient expectation of the happy hour wherein we may meet again; but if death have made the separation, as some time or

other it must, this occasions a grief scarce to be paralleled by all the misfortunes of human life, and wherein we may pay dear enough for the comforts of our friendship. But oh! how happy are those who have placed their love on him who can never be absent from them! They need but open their eyes, and they shall everywhere behold the traces of his presence and glory, and converse with him whom their soul loveth, and this makes the darkest prison or wildest desert not only supportable, but delightful to them.

The divine love makes us partake of an infinite happiness
In fine, a lover is miserable, if the person whom he loveth be so; they who have made an exchange of hearts by love get thereby an interest in one another's happiness and misery; and this makes love a troublesome passion, when placed on earth. The most fortunate person hath grief enough to mar the tranquillity of his friend, and it is hard to hold it out, when we are attacked on all hands, and suffer not only in our own person, but in another's. But if God were the object of our love, we should share it in infinite happiness without any mixture of possibility of diminution; we should rejoice to behold the glory of God, and receive comfort and pleasure from all the praises wherewith men and angels do extol him. It should delight us beyond all expression, to consider that the beloved of our souls is infinitely happy in himself, and that

all his enemies can not shake or unsettle his throne, 'that our God is in the heavens, and doth whatsoever he pleaseth'.

Behold on what sure foundation his happiness is built whose soul is possessed with divine love, whose will is transformed into the will of God, and whose greatest desire is, that his Maker should be pleased! Oh! the peace, the rest, the satisfaction that attendeth such a temper of mind!

He that loveth God finds sweetness in every dispensation
What an infinite pleasure must it needs be, thus, as it were, to lose ourselves in him, and being swallowed up in the overcoming sense of his goodness, to offer ourselves a living sacrifice always ascending unto him in flames of love. Never doth a soul know what solid joy and substantial pleasure is, till once, being weary of itself, it renounce all propriety, give itself up unto the Author of its being, and feel itself become a hallowed and devoted thing, and can say, from an inward sense and feeling: 'My beloved is mine'. I account all his interest mine own, 'and I am his'. I am content to be any thing for him, and care not for myself, but that I may serve him.

A person moulded into this temper would find pleasure in all the dispensations of Providence: temporal enjoyments would have another relish, when he should taste the divine goodness in them, and consider them as tokens of love sent by his dearest Lord and Maker; and chastisements, though they be not joyous but grievous, would hereby lose their sting, the rod as well as the staff would comfort him - he would snatch a kiss from the hand that was smiting him, and gather sweetness from that severity - nay, he would rejoice that though God did not the will of such a worthless and foolish creatures as himself, yet he did his own will, and accomplished his own designs, which are infinitely more holy and wise.

The duties of religion are delightful to him

The exercises of religion, which to others are insipid and tedious, do yield the highest pleasure and delight to souls possessed with divine love; they rejoice when they are called 'to go up to the house of the Lord, that they may see his power and his glory, as they have formerly seen it in the sanctuary' (Psalm 63:2). They never think themselves so happy as when, having retired from the world, and gotten free from the noise and hurry of affairs, and silenced all their clamorous passions, those troublesome guests within, they have placed themselves in the presence of God, and entertain fellowship and communion with him; they delight to adore his perfections and recount his favours, and to protest their affection to him, and tell him a thousand times that they love him, to lay out their troubles or wants before him, and disburden their hearts in his bosom.

Repentance itself is a delightful exercise when it floweth from the principle of love: there is a secret sweetness which accompanieth those tears of remorse, those meltings and relentings of a soul returning unto God, and lamenting its former unkindness.

The severities of a holy life, and that constant watch which we are obliged to keep over our hearts and ways, are very troublesome to those who are only ruled and acted by an external law, and have no law in their minds inclining them to the performance of their duty; but where divine love possesseth the soul, it stands as sentinel to keep out every thing that may offend the beloved, and doth disdainfully repulse those temptations which assault it; it complieth cheerfully, not only with explicit commands, but with the most secret notices of the beloved's pleasure, and is ingenious in discovering what will be most grateful and acceptable unto him; it makes mortification and self-denial change their harsh and dreadful names and become easy, sweet and delightful things.

But I find this part of my letter swell bigger than I designed; indeed, who would not be tempted to dwell on so pleasant a theme. I shall endeavour to compensate it by brevity in the other points.

The excellency of charity

The next branch of the Divine life is a universal charity and love. The excellency of this grace will be easily acknowledged; for what can be more noble and generous than a heart enlarged to embrace the whole world, whose wishes and designs are levelled at the good and welfare of the universe, which considereth every man's interest as his own? He who loveth his neighbour as himself can never entertain any base or injurious thought, or be wanting in expressions of bounty; he had rather suffer a thousand wrongs than be guilty of one, and never accounts himself happy, but when some one or other hath been benefited by him: the malice or ingratitude of men is not able to resist his love; he overlooks their injuries, and pities their folly, and overcomes their evil with good, and never designs any other revenge against his most bitter and malicious enemies than to put all the obligations he can upon them, whether they will or not. Is it any wonder that such a person be reverenced and admired, and accounted the darling of mankind? This inward goodness and benignity of spirit reflects a certain sweetness and serenity upon the very countenance, and makes it amiable and lovely; it inspireth the soul with a noble resolution and courage, and makes it capable of enterprising and effecting the highest of things.

Those heroic actions which we are wont to read with admiration, have, for the most part, been the effects of the love of one's own country, or of particular friendship; and certainly a more extensive and universal affection must be much more powerful and efficacious.

The pleasure that attends it

Again, as charity flows from a noble and excellent temper, so it is accompanied with the greatest satisfaction and pleasure; it delights the soul to feel itself thus enlarged, and to be delivered from those disquieting as well as deformed passions, malice, hatred, and envy, and become gentle, sweet and benign. Had I my choice of all things that may tend to my present felicity, I would pitch upon this - to have my heart possessed with the greatest kindness and affection towards all men in the world. I am sure this would make me partake in all the happiness of others - their inward endowments and outward prosperity; every thing that did benefit and advantage them would afford me comfort and pleasure; and though I should frequently meet with occasions of grief and compassion, yet there is a sweetness in commiseration, which makes it infinitely more desirable than a stupid insensibility; and the consideration of that infinite goodness and wisdom which governs the world might repress any excessive trouble for particular calamities that happen in it, and the hopes or possibility of men's after-happiness might moderate their sorrow for their present misfortunes.

Certainly, next to the love and enjoyment of God, that ardent charity and affection wherewith blessed souls do embrace one another is justly to be reckoned as the greatest felicity of those regions above; and did it universally prevail in the world, it would anticipate that blessedness, and make us taste of the joys of heaven upon earth.

The excellency of purity

That which I named as a third branch of religion was purity, and you may remember I described it to consist in a contempt of sensual pleasures, and a resoluteness to undergo those troubles and pains we may meet with in the performance of our duty. Now, the naming of this may suffice to recommend it as a most noble and excellent quality. There is no slavery so base as that whereby a man becomes a drudge to his own lusts, or any victory so glorious as that which is obtained over them. Never can that person be capable of any thing that is noble and worthy, who is sunk in the gross and feculent pleasures of sense, or bewitched with the light and airy gratifications of fancy; but the religious soul is of a more sublime and divine temper; it knows it was made for higher things, and scorns to step aside one foot out of the ways of holiness for the obtaining of any of these.

The delight it affords

And this purity is accompanied with a great deal of pleasure: whatsoever defiles the soul disturbs it too: all impure delights have a sting in them, and leave smart and trouble behind them. Excess and intemperance, and all inordinate lusts, are so much enemies to the health of the body, and the interests of this present life, that a little consideration might oblige any rational man to forbear them on that very score; and if the religious person go higher, and do not only abstain from noxious pleasures, but neglect those that are innocent, this is not to be looked upon as any violent or uneasy restraint, but as the effect of better choice, that their minds are taken up in the pursuit of more sublime and refined delights, so that they can not be concerned in these. Any person that is engaged in a violent and passionate affection will easily forget his ordinary gratifications, will be little curious about his diet or his bodily ease, or to divertisement he was wonted to delight in. No wonder, then, if souls overpowered with divine love despise inferior pleasures, and be almost ready to grudge the body its necessary attendance for the common accommodations of life, judging all these impertinent to their main happiness, and those higher enjoyments they are pursuing.

As for the hardships they may meet with, they rejoice in them as opportunities to exercise and testify their affection; and since they are able to do so little for God, they are glad of the honour to suffer for him.

The excellency of humility

The last branch of religion is humility; and however, to vulgar and carnal eyes, this may appear an abject, base, and despicable quality, yet really the soul of man is not capable of a higher and more noble endowment. It is a silly ignorance that begets pride; but humility arises from a nearer acquaintance with excellent things, which keeps men from doating on trifles, or admiring themselves because of some petty attainments.

Noble and well-educated souls have no such high opinion of riches, beauty, strength, and other such like advantages, as to value themselves for them, or despise those that want them: and as for inward worth and real goodness, the sense they have of the divine perfections makes them think very meanly of any thing they have hitherto attained, and be still endeavouring to surmount themselves, and make nearer approaches to those infinite excellencies which they admire.

I know not what thoughts people may have of humility, but I see almost every person pretending to it, and shunning such expressions and actions as may make them be accounted arrogant and presumptuous, so that those who are most desirous of praise will be loth to commend themselves. What are all those compliments and modes of civility, so frequent in our ordinary converse, but so many protestations of the esteem of others, and the low thoughts we have of ourselves? and must not that humility be a noble and excellent endowment when the very shadows of it are accounted so necessary a part of good breeding?

The pleasure and sweetness of a humble temper
Again, the grace is accompanied with a great deal of happiness and tranquillity: the proud and arrogant person is a trouble to all that converse with him, but most of all unto himself: every thing is enough to vex him; but scarce any thing sufficient to content and please him. He is ready to quarrel with every thing that falls out; as if he himself were such a considerable person that God Almighty should do every thing to gratify him, and all the creatures of heaven and earth should wait upon him, and obey his will.

The leaves of high trees do shake with every blast of wind; and every breath, every evil word, will disquiet and torment an arrogant man; but the humble person hath the advantage, when he is despised, that none can think more meanly of him than he doth of himself; and therefore he is not troubled at the matter, but can easily bear those reproaches which wound the other to the soul. And withal, as he is less affected with injuries, so indeed he is less obnoxious unto them: 'Contention, which cometh of pride', betrays a man into a thousand inconveniencies, which those of a meek and lowly temper seldom meet with. True and genuine humility begetteth both a veneration and love among all wise and discerning persons, while pride defeateth its own design, and depriveth a man of that honour it makes him pretend to.

But, as the 'chief exercises of humility' are those which relate unto Almighty God, so these are accompanied with the greatest satisfaction and sweetness. It is impossible to express the great pleasure and delight which religious persons feel in the lowest prostration of their souls before God, when, having a deep sense of the divine majesty and glory, they sink, if I may so speak, to the bottom of their beings, and vanish and disappear in the presence of God, by a serious and affectionate acknowledgment of their own nothingness, and the shortness and imperfections of their attainments; when they understand the full sense and emphasis of the Psalmist's exclamation, 'Lord, what is man?' and can utter it with the same affection. Never did any haughty and ambitious person receive the praises and applauses of men with so much pleasure as the humble and religious do renounce them: 'Not unto us, O Lord, not unto us, but unto thy name give glory', etc.

Thus I have spoken something of the excellencies and advantage of religion in its several branches; but should be very injurious to the subject, did I pretend to have given any perfect account of it. Let us acquaint ourselves with it, my dear friend, let us acquaint ourselves with it, and experience will teach us more than all that ever hath been spoken or written concerning it. But if we may suppose the soul to be already awakened unto some longing desires after so great a blessedness, it will be good to give them vent, and suffer them to issue forth in some such aspirations as these.

A Prayer

Good God! what a mighty felicity is this to which we are called? How graciously hast thou joined our duty and happiness together, and prescribed that for our work, the performance whereof is a great reward! And shall such silly worms be advanced to so great a height? Wilt thou allow us to raise our eyes to thee? Wilt thou admit and accept our affection? Shall we receive the impression of thy divine excellencies by beholding and admiring them, and partake of thy infinite blessedness and glory by loving thee, and rejoicing in them?

Oh! the happiness of those souls that have broken the fetters of self-love, and disentangled their affection from every narrow and peculiar good, whose understandings are enlightened by the Holy Spirit, and their wills enlarged to the extent of thine, who love thee above all things, and all mankind for thy sake!

I am persuaded, O God, I am persuaded that I can never be happy, till my carnal and corrupt affections be mortified, and the pride and vanity of my spirit be subdued, and till I come seriously to despise the world, and think nothing of myself.

But, oh! when shall it once be! Oh! when wilt thou come unto me and satisfy my soul with thy likeness, making me holy as thou art holy, even in all manner of conversation! Hast thou given me a prospect of so great a felicity, and wilt thou not bring me unto it? Hast thou excited these desires in my soul, and wilt thou not also satisfy them?

Oh! teach me to do thy will, for thou art my God, thy Spirit is good, lead me unto the land of uprightness. Quicken me, O Lord, for thy name's sake, and perfect that which concerneth me: thy mercy, O Lord, endureth for ever, forsake not the works of thine own hands.

Part 3

The Despondent Thoughts of Some Newly
Awakened to a Right Sense of Things

~~~~~~

I have hitherto considered wherein true religion
doth consist, and how desirable a thing it is; but
when one sees how infinitely distant the common temper and frame of men is from it, he may
perhaps be ready to despond, and give over, and
think it utterly impossible to be attained: he may
sit down in sadness, and bemoan himself, and say
in the anguish and bitterness of his spirit: 'They
are happy indeed whose souls are awakened unto
the divine life; who are thus renewed in the spirit
of their minds; but alas! I am quite of another
constitution, and am not able to effect so mighty a
change: if outward observances could have done
the business, I might have hoped to acquit myself
by diligence and care; but since nothing but a new
nature can serve the turn, what am I able to do? I
could bestow all my goods in oblations to God, or
alms to the poor, but cannot command that love
and charity, without which this expense would
profit me nothing (1 Corinthians 13:3).

'This gift of God can not be purchased with money (Acts 8:20); if a man should give all the substance of his house for love, it would utterly be contemned (Song of Solomon 8:7); I could pine and macerate my body, and undergo many hardships and troubles; but I cannot get all my corruptions starved, nor my affections wholly weaned from earthly things: there is still some worldly desires lurking in my heart, and those vanities that I have shut out of the doors are always getting in by the windows. I am many times convinced of my own meanness, of the weakness of my body, and the far greater weakness of my soul; but this doth rather beget indignation and discontent, than true humility in my spirit; and though I should come to think meanly of myself, yet I cannot endure that others should think so too.

'In a word, when I reflect on my highest and most specious attainments, I have reason to suspect, that they are all but the effects of nature, the issues of self-love acting under several disguises; and this principle is so powerful, and so deeply rooted in me, that I can never hope to be delivered from the dominion of it. I may toss and turn as a door on the hinges, but can never get clear off, or be quite unhinged of self, which is still the centre of all my motions; so that all the advantage I can draw from the discovery of religion is but to see, at a huge distance, that felicity which I am not able to reach; like a man in shipwreck, who discerns the land, and envies the happiness of those who are there, but thinks it impossible for himself to get ashore.'

The unreasonableness of these fears

These, I say, or such like desponding thoughts, may arise in the minds of those persons who begin to conceive somewhat more of the nature and excellency of religion than before; they have spied the land, and seen that it is exceedingly good, that it floweth with milk and honey: but they find they have the children of Anak to grapple with, many powerful lusts and corruptions to overcome, and they fear they shall never prevail against them.

But, why should we give way to such discouraging suggestions? Why should we entertain such unreasonable fears, which damp our spirits, and weaken our hands, and augment the difficulties of our way?

Let us encourage ourselves my dear friend, let us encourage ourselves with those mighty aids we are to expect in this spiritual warfare, for greater is he that is for us than all that can rise up against us; 'The eternal God is our refuge and underneath are the everlasting arms' (Deuteronomy 33:27).

Let us be strong in the Lord, and the power of his might, for he it is that shall tread down our enemies: God hath a tender regard unto the souls of men, and is infinitely willing to promote their welfare; he hath condescended to our weakness, and declared with an oath, that he hath no pleasure in our destruction.

There is no such thing as despite or envy lodged in the bosom of that ever-blessed Being, whose name and nature is Love. He created us at first in a happy condition, and now when we are fallen from it, 'He hath laid help upon one that is mighty to save' (Psalm 89:19), hath committed the care of our souls to no meaner person than the eternal Son of his love. It is he that is the captain of our salvation, and what enemies can be too strong for us, when we are fighting under his banner?

Did not the Son of God come down from the bosom of his Father, and pitch his tabernacle among the sons of men, that he might recover and propagate the divine life, and restore the image of God in their souls? All the mighty works which he performed, all the sad afflictions which he sustained, had this for their scope and design; for this did he labour and toil, for this did he bleed and die; 'He was with child, he was in pain, and hath he brought forth nothing but wind, hath he wrought no deliverance in the earth? (Isaiah 26:18).

Shall he not see of the travail of his soul' (Isaiah 53:11)? Certainly it is impossible that this great contrivance of heaven should prove abortive, that such a mighty undertaking should fail and miscarry: it hath already been effectual for the salvation of many thousands, who were once as far from the kingdom of heaven as we can suppose ourselves to be, and our 'High priest continueth for ever, and is able to save them to the uttermost that come unto God by him' (Hebrews 7:24, 25); he is tender and compassionate, he knoweth our infirmities, and had experience of our temptations, 'A bruised reed will he not break, and smoking flax will he not quench, till he send forth judgment unto victory' (Matthew 12:20).

He hath sent out his Holy Spirit, whose sweet but powerful breathings are still moving up and down in the world, to quicken and revive the souls of men, and awaken them unto the sense and feeling of those divine things for which they were made, and is ready to assist such weak and languishing creatures as we are, in our essays towards holiness and felicity; and when once it hath taken hold of a soul, and kindled in it the smallest spark of divine love, it will be sure to preserve and cherish, and bring it forth into a flame, 'which many waters shall not quench, neither shall the floods be able to drown it' (Song of Solomon 8:7).

Whenever this day begins to dawn, 'and the daystar to arise in the heart' (2 Peter 1:19), it will easily dispel the powers of darkness, and make ignorance and folly, and all the corrupt and selfish affections of men, flee away as fast as the shades of night, when the sun cometh out of his chamber, for 'the path of the just is as the shining light, which shineth more and more unto the perfect day (Proverbs 4:18). They shall go on from strength to strength till every one of them appear before God in Zion (Psalm 84:7).

Why should we think it impossible that true goodness and universal love should ever come to sway and prevail in our souls? Is not this their primitive state and condition, their native and genuine constitution as they came first from the hands of their Maker? Sin and corruption are but usurpers, and though they have long kept the possession, yet 'from the beginning it was not so'. That inordinate self-love, which one would think were rooted in our very being, and interwoven with the constitution of our nature, is nevertheless of foreign extraction, and had no place at all in the state of integrity. We have still so much reason left as to condemn it; our understandings are easily convinced, that we ought to be wholly devoted to him from whom we have our being, and to love him infinitely more than ourselves, who is infinitely better than we; and our wills would readily comply with this, if they were not disordered and put out of tune: and is not he who made our souls able to rectify and mend them again? shall we not be able, by his assistance, to vanquish and expel those violent intruders, 'and turn unto flight the armies of the aliens' (Hebrews 11:34)?

No sooner shall we take up arms in this holy war, but we shall have all the saints on earth, and all the angels in heaven, engaged on our party; the holy Church throughout the world is daily interceding with God for the success of all such endeavours; and doubtless, those heavenly hosts above are nearly concerned in the interests of religion, and infinitely desirous to see the divine life thriving and prevailing in this inferior world; and that the will of God may be done by us on earth, as it is done by themselves in heaven: and may we not then encourage ourselves, as the prophet did his servant, when he showed him the horses and chariots of fire, 'Fear not, for they that be with us, are more than they that be against us' (2 Kings 6:16, 17).

We must do what we can, and depend on the divine assistance
Away then with all perplexing fears and desponding thoughts: to undertake vigorously, and rely confidently on the divine assistance, is more than half the conquest, 'Let us arise and be doing, and the LORD will be with us' (1 Chronicles 22:16).

It is true, religion in the souls of men is the immediate work of God, and all our natural endeavours can neither produce it alone, nor merit those supernatural aids by which it must be wrought: the Holy Ghost must come upon us, and the power of the Highest must overshadow us, before that holy thing can be begotten, and

Christ be formed in us: but yet we must not expect that this whole work should be done without any concurring endeavours of our own: we must not lie loitering in the ditch, and wait till Omnipotence pull us from thence; no, no! we must bestir ourselves, and actuate those powers which we have already received: we must put forth ourselves to our utmost capacities, and then we may hope that, 'our labour shall not be in vain in the Lord' (1 Corinthians 15:58).

All the art and industry of man cannot form the smallest herb, or make a stalk of corn to grow in the field; it is the energy of nature, and the influences of heaven, which produce this effect; it is God 'who causeth the grass to grow, and herb for the service of man' (Psalm 104:14); and yet nobody will say that the labours of the husbandman are useless or unnecessary: so, likewise, the human soul is immediately created by God; it is he who both formeth and enliveneth the child; and yet he hath appointed the marriage-bed as the ordinary means for the propagation of mankind. Though there must intervene a stroke of Omnipotence to effect this mighty change in our souls, yet ought we to do what we can to fit and prepare ourselves, for we must break up our fallow ground, and root out the weeds, and pull up the thorns (Jeremiah 4:3), that so we may be more ready to receive the seeds of grace, and the dew of heaven.

It is true, God hath been found of some who sought him not; he hath cast himself in their way, who were quite out of his; he hath laid hold upon them, and stopped their course upon a sudden; for so was St Paul converted in his journey to Damascus. But certainly this is not God's ordinary method of dealing with men: though he hath not tied himself to means, yet he hath tied us to the use of them; and we have never more reason to expect the divine assistance, than when we are doing our utmost endeavours.

It shall therefore be my next work to show what course we ought to take for attaining that blessed temper I have hitherto described. But here, if in delivering my own thoughts, I shall chance to differ from what is or may be said by others in this matter, I would not be thought to contradict and oppose them, more than physicians do, when they prescribe several remedies for the same disease, which perhaps are all useful and good. Every one may propose the method he judges most proper and convenient, but he doth not thereby pretend that the cure can never be effected unless that be exactly observed.

I doubt it hath occasioned much unnecessary disquietude to some holy persons, that they have not found such a regular and orderly transaction in their souls as they have seen described in books; that they have not passed through all those steps and stages of conversion which some 'who, perhaps, have felt themselves, have too peremptorily' prescribed unto others: God hath several ways of dealing with the souls of men, and it sufficeth if the work be accomplished, whatever the methods have been.

Again, though in proposing directions, I must follow that order which the nature of things shall lead to; yet I do not mean that the same method should be so punctually observed in the practice, as if the latter rules were never to be heeded till some considerable time have been spent in practising the former: the directions I intend are mutually conducive one to another, and are all to be performed as occasion shall serve, and we find ourselves enabled to perform them.

We must shun all manner of sin

But now that I may detain you no longer, if we desire to have our souls moulded to this holy frame, to become partakers of the divine nature, and have Christ formed in our hearts, we must seriously resolve, and carefully endeavour, to avoid and abandon all vicious and sinful practices.

There can be no treaty of peace till once we lay down these weapons of rebellion wherewith we fight against heaven; nor can we expect to have our distempers cured if we be daily feeding on poison. Every wilful sin gives a mortal wound to the soul, and puts it at a greater distance from God and goodness; and we can never hope to have our hearts purified from corrupt affections, unless we cleanse our hands from vicious actions.

Now, in this case, we cannot excuse ourselves by the pretence of impossibility; for sure our outward man is some way in our power; we have some command of our feet, and hands, and tongue, nay, and of our thoughts and fancies too, at least so far as to divert them from impure and sinful objects, and to turn our mind another way: and we should find this power and authority much strengthened and advanced if we were careful to manage and exercise it. In the mean while, I acknowledge our corruptions are so strong, and our temptations so many, that it will require a great deal of steadfastness and resolution, of watchfulness and care, to preserve ourselves, even in this degree of innocence and purity.

We must know what things are sinful

And, first, let us inform ourselves well what those sins are from which we ought to abstain. And here we must not take our measures from the maxims of the world, or the practices of those whom in charity we call good men. Most people have very light apprehensions of these things, and are not sensible of any fault, unless it be gross and flagitious, and scarce reckon any so great as that which they call preciseness: and those who are more serious, do many times allow themselves too great latitude and freedom.

Alas! how much pride and vanity, and passion, and humour, how much weakness and folly, and sin, doth every day show itself in their converse and behaviour? It may be they are humbled for it, and striving against it, and are daily gaining some ground; but then the progress is so small, and their failing so many, that we had need to choose an exacter pattern.

Every one of us must answer for himself, and the practices of others will never warrant and secure us. It is the highest folly to regulate our actions by any other standard than that by which they must be judged. If ever we would 'cleanse our way', it must be 'by taking heed thereto according to the word of God' (Psalm 119:9): and that 'word which is quick, and powerful, and sharper than any two-edged sword, piercing even to the dividing asunder of soul and spirit, and of the joints and marrow, and is a discerner of the thoughts and intents of the heart' (Hebrews 4:12) will certainly discover many things to be sinful and heinous which pass for very innocent in the eyes of the world.

Let us therefore imitate the Psalmist, who saith, 'Concerning the works of men, by the words of thy lips I have kept myself from the paths of the destroyer' (Psalm 17:4).

Let us acquaint ourselves with the strict and holy laws of our religion: let us consider the discourses of our blessed Saviour, especially that divine sermon on the mount, and the writings of his holy apostles, where an ingenuous and unbiased mind may clearly discern those limits and bounds by which our actions ought to be confined: and then let us never look upon any sin as light and inconsiderable; but be fully persuaded, that the smallest is infinitely heinous in the sight of God, and prejudicial to the soul of men: and that if we had the right sense of things, we should be as deeply affected with the least irregularities as now we are with the highest crimes.

We must resist the temptations to sin, by considering the evils they will draw on us

But now, amongst those things which we discover to be sinful, there will be some unto which, through the disposition of our nature, or long custom, or the endearments of pleasure, we are so much wedded, that it will be like cutting off the right hand, or pulling out the right eye, to abandon them. But must we therefore sit down and wait till all difficulties be over, and every temptation be gone? This were to imitate the fool in the poet, who stood the whole day at the river-side, till all the water should run by. We must not indulge our inclinations, as we do little children, till they grow weary of the thing they are unwilling to let go. We must not continue our sinful practices, in hopes that the divine grace will one day overpower our spirits, and make us hate them for their own deformity.

Let us suppose the worst, that we are utterly destitute of any supernatural principle, and want that taste by which we should discern and abhor perverse things; yet sure we are capable of some considerations which may be of force to persuade us to this reformation of our lives. If the inward deformity and heinous nature of sin cannot affect us, at least we may be frighted by those dreadful consequences that attend it: that same selfish principle which pusheth us forward unto the pursuit of sinful pleasures, will make us loth to buy them at the rate of everlasting misery.

Thus, we may encounter self-love with its own weapons, and employ one natural inclination for repressing the exorbitances of another. Let us therefore accustom ourselves to consider seriously, what a fearful thing it must needs be to irritate and offend that infinite Being on whom we hang and depend every moment, who needs but to withdraw his mercies to make us miserable, or his assistance to make us nothing.

Let us frequently remember the shortness and uncertainty of our lives, and how that, after we have taken a few turns more in the world, and conversed a little longer amongst men, we must all go down into the dark and silent grave, and carry nothing along with us but anguish and regret for all our sinful enjoyments; and then think what horror must needs seize the guilty soul, to find itself naked and all alone before the severe and impartial Judge of the world, to render an exact account, not only of its more important and considerable transactions, but of every word that the tongue hath uttered, and the swiftest and most secret thought that ever passed through the mind.

Let us sometimes represent to ourselves the terrors of that dreadful day, when the foundation of the earth shall be shaken, and the heavens shall pass away with a great noise, and the elements shall melt with fervent heat, and the present frame of nature be dissolved (2 Peter 3:10), and our eyes shall see the blessed Jesus, who came once into the world in all humility to visit us, to purchase pardon for us, and beseech us to accept of it, now appearing in the majesty of his glory, and descending from heaven in a flaming fire, to take vengeance on those that have despised his mercy, and persisted in rebellion against him; when all the hidden things of darkness should be brought to light, and the counsels of the heart shall be made manifest (1 Corinthians 4:5): when those secret impurities and subtile frauds, whereof the world did never suspect us, shall be exposed and laid open to public view, and many thousand actions which we never dreamed to be sinful, or else had altogether forgotten, shall be charged home upon our consciences, with such evident convictions of guilt, that we shall neither be able to deny nor excuse them.

Then shall all the angels in heaven, and all the saints that ever lived on the earth, approve that dreadful sentence which shall be passed on wicked men; and those who, perhaps, did love and esteem them when they lived in the world, shall look upon them with indignation and abhorrence, and never make one request for their deliverance.

Let us consider the eternal punishment of damned souls, which are shadowed forth in scripture by metaphors taken from those things that are most terrible and grievous in the world, and yet all do not suffice to convey unto our minds any full apprehensions of them. When we have joined together the importance of all these expressions, and added unto them whatever our fancy can conceive of misery and torment, we must still remember, that all this comes infinitely short of the truth and reality of the thing.

'Tis true, this is a sad and melancholy subject; there is anguish and horror in the consideration of it; but sure, it must be infinitely more dreadful to endure it: and such thoughts as these may be very useful to fright us from the courses that would lead us thither; how fond soever we may be of sinful pleasures, the fear of hell would make us abstain: our most forward inclinations will startle and give back, when pressed with that question in the prophet, 'Who amongst us can dwell with everlasting burnings?' (Isaiah 33:14).

To this very purpose it is that the terrors of another world are so frequently represented in holy writ, and that in such terms as are most proper to affect and influence a carnal mind: these fears can never suffice to make any person truly good; but certainly they may restrain us from much evil, and have often made way for more ingenuous and kindly impressions.

We must keep a constant watch over ourselves

But it will not suffice to consider these things once and again, nor to form some resolutions of abandoning our sins, unless we maintain a constant guard, and be continually watching against them. Sometimes the mind is awakened to see the dismal consequences of a vicious life, and straight we are resolved to reform; but alas! it presently falleth asleep, and we lose that prospect which we had of things, and then temptations take the advantage; they solicit and importune us continually, and so do frequently engage our consent before we are aware. It is the folly and ruin of most people to live at adventure, and take part in every thing that comes in their way, seldom considering what they are about to say or do.

If we would have our resolutions take effect, we must take heed unto our ways, and set a

watch before the door of our lips, and examine
the motions that arise in our hearts, and cause
them to tell whence they come, and whither
they go; whether it be pride or passion, or any
corrupt and vicious humour, that prompteth
us to any design, and whether God will be of-
fended, or any body harmed by it.

And if we have no time for long reasonings,
let us, at least, turn our eyes toward God, and
place ourselves in his presence, to ask his leave
and approbation for what we do: let us consider
ourselves under the all-seeing eye of that divine
Majesty, as in the midst of an infinite globe of
light, which compasseth us about both behind
and before, and pierceth to the innermost cor-
ners of our soul.

The sense and remembrance of the divine
presence is the most ready and effectual means,
both to discover what is unlawful, and to restrain
us from it. There are some things a person
could make shift to palliate or defend, and yet
he dares not look Almighty God in the face and
adventure upon them.

If we look unto him, we shall be lightened;
'if we set him always before us, he will guide us
by his eye, and instruct us in the way wherein
we ought to walk'.

We must often examine our actions
This care and watchfulness over our actions
must be seconded by frequent and serious

reflections upon them, not only that we may obtain the divine mercy and pardon for our sins, by an humble and sorrowful acknowledgment of them; but also that we may reinforce and strengthen our resolutions, and learn to decline or resist the temptations by which we have been formerly foiled.

It is an advice worthy of a Christian, though it did first drop from a heathen pen, that before we betake ourselves to rest, we renew and examine all the passages of the day, that we may have the comfort of what we have done aright, and may redress what we find to have been amiss, and make the shipwrecks of one day be as marks to direct our course in another.

This may be called the very art of virtuous living, and would contribute wonderfully to advance our reformation, and preserve our innocence. But, withal, we must not forget to implore the divine assistance, especially against those sins that do most easily beset us: and though it be supposed that our hearts are not yet moulded into that spiritual frame which should render our devotions acceptable; yet, methinks, such considerations as have been proposed to deter us from sin, may also stir us up to some natural seriousness, and make our prayers against it as earnest, at least, as they are wont to be against other calamities; and I doubt not but God, who heareth the cry of the ravens, will have some regard even to such petitions as proceed from those natural passions which himself hath implanted in us: besides that those prayers against sin will be powerful engagements on ourselves to excite us to watchfulness and care; and common ingenuity will make us ashamed to relapse into those faults which we have lately bewailed before God, and against which we have begged his assistance.

It is fit to restrain ourselves in many lawful things

Thus are we to make the first essay for recovering the divine life, by restraining the natural inclinations, that they break not out into sinful practices. But now I must add, that Christian prudence will teach us to abstain from gratifications that are not simply unlawful, and that not only that we may secure our innocence, which would be in continual hazard, if we should strain our liberty to the utmost point; but also, that hereby we may weaken the forces of nature, and teach our appetites to obey.

We must do with ourselves as prudent parents with their children, who cross their wills in many little indifferent things, to make them manageable and submissive in more considerable instances.

He who would mortify the pride and vanity of his spirit should stop his ears to the most deserved praises, and sometimes forbear his just vindication from the censures and aspersions of others, especially if they reflect only upon his prudence and conduct, and not on his virtue and innocence.

He who would check a revengeful humour, would do well to deny himself the satisfaction of representing unto others the injuries which he hath sustained; and if we would so take heed to our ways that we sin not with our tongue, we must accustom ourselves much to solitude and silence, and sometimes, with the Psalmist, 'Hold our peace even from good', till once we have gotten some command over that unruly member. Thus, I say, we may bind up our natural inclinations, and make our appetites more moderate in their craving, by accustoming them to frequent refusals; but it is not enough to have them under violence and restraint.

We must strive to put ourselves out of love with the world
Our next essay must be, to wean our affections from created things, and all the delights and entertainments of the lower life, which sink and depress the souls of men, and retard their motions toward God and heaven; and this we must do by possessing our minds with a deep persuasion of the vanity and emptiness of worldly enjoyments.

This is an ordinary theme, and everybody can make declamations upon it; but alas! how few understand and believe what they say? These notions float in our brains, and come sliding off our tongues, but we have no deep impression of

them on our spirits; we feel not the truth which
we pretend to believe. We can tell that all the
glory and splendour, all the pleasures and enjoyments of the world are vanity and nothing;
and yet these nothings take up all our thoughts,
and engross all our affections, they stifle the
better inclinations of our soul, and inveigle us
into many a sin.

It may be, in a sober mood, we give them the
slight, and resolve to be no longer deluded with
them; but these thoughts seldom outlive the
next temptation; the vanities which we have
shut out at the door get in at a postern; there
are still some pretensions, some hopes that
flatter us; and after we have been frustrated
a thousand times, we must continually be repeating the experiment: the least difference of
circumstances is enough to delude us, and make
us expect that satisfaction in one thing which
we have missed in another; but could we once
get clearly off, and come to a real and serious
contempt of worldly things, this were a very
considerable advancement in our way.

The soul of man is of a vigorous and active
nature, and hath in it a raging and unextinguish-
able thirst, an immaterial kind of fire, always
catching at some object or other, in conjunction
wherewith it thinks to be happy; and were it
once rent from the world, and all the bewitch-
ing enjoyments under the sun, it would quickly
search after some higher and more excellent

object, to satisfy its ardent and importunate cravings; and being no longer dazzled with glittering vanities, would fix on that supreme and all-sufficient Good, where it would discover such beauty and sweetness as would charm and overpower all its affections.

The love of the world, and the love of God, are like the scales of a balance, as the one falleth, the other doth rise: when our natural inclinations prosper, and the creature is exalted in our soul, religion is faint, and doth languish; but when earthly objects wither away, and lose their beauty, and the soul begins to cool and flag in its prosecution of them, then the seeds of grace take root, and the divine life begins to flourish and prevail.

It doth, therefore, nearly concern us, to convince ourselves of the emptiness and vanity of creature-enjoyments, and reason our hearts out of love with them: let us seriously consider all that our reason, or our faith, or our own experience, or the observation of others, can suggest to this effect; let us ponder the matter over and over, and fix our thoughts on this truth, till we become really persuaded of it.

Amidst all our pursuits and designs, let us stop and ask ourselves, For what end is all this? At what do I aim? Can the gross and muddy pleasures of sense, or a heap of white and yellow earth, or the esteem and affection of silly creatures, like myself, satisfy a rational and

immortal soul? Have I not tried these things
already? Will they have a higher relish, and
yield me more contentment tomorrow than
yesterday, or the next year than they did the
last? There may be some little difference betwixt
that which I am now pursuing, and that which
I enjoyed before; but sure, my former enjoyments did show as pleasant, and promised as
fair, before I attained them; like the rainbow,
they looked very glorious at a distance, but when
I approached, I found nothing but emptiness
and vapour. Oh! what a poor thing would the
life of man be, if it were capable of no higher
enjoyment.

I cannot insist on this subject; and there is
the less need when I remember to whom I am
writing. Yes, my dear friend, you have had as
great experience of the emptiness and vanity
of human things, and have, at present, as few
worldly engagements as any that I know. I
have sometimes reflected on those passages
of your life wherewith you have been pleased
to acquaint me; and methinks, through all, I
can discern a design of the divine providence
to wean your affections from every thing here
below. The trials you have had of those things
which the world doats upon, have taught you to
despise them; and you have found, by experience, that neither the endowments of nature,
nor the advantages of fortune, are sufficient for
happiness; that every rose hath its thorn, and

there may be a worm at the root of the fairest gourd; some secret and undiscerned grief, which may make a person deserve the pity of those who, perhaps, do admire or envy their supposed felicity.

If any earthly comforts have got too much of your heart, I think they have been your relations and friends; and the dearest of these are removed out of the world, so that you must raise your mind toward heaven when you would think upon them. Thus God hath provided that your heart may be loosed from the world, and that he may not have any rival in your affection, which I have always observed to be so large and unbounded, so noble and disinterested, that no inferior object can answer or deserve it.

We must do those outward actions that are commanded
When we have got our corruptions restrained, and our natural appetites and inclinations toward worldly things in some measure subdued, we must proceed to such exercises as have a more immediate tendency to excite and awaken the divine life. And first, let us endeavour conscientiously to perform those duties which religion doth require, and whereunto it would incline us, if it did prevail in our souls.

If we cannot get our inward disposition presently changed, let us study, at least, to regulate our outward deportment. If our hearts be not yet inflamed with divine love, let us, however, own our allegiance to that infinite Majesty, by attending his service, and listening to his Word, by speaking reverently of his name, and praising his goodness, and exhorting others to serve and obey him.

If we want that charity, and those bowels of compassion which we ought to have toward our neighbours, yet must we not omit any occasion of doing them good; if our hearts be haughty and proud, we must nevertheless, study a modest and humble deportment.

These external performances are of little value in themselves, yet may they help us forward to better things: the Apostle indeed telleth us, 'that bodily exercise profiteth little'; but he seems not to affirm that it is altogether useless: it is always good to be doing what we can, for then God is wont to pity our weakness, and assist our feeble endeavours; and when true charity and humility, and other graces of the divine Spirit, come to take root in our souls, they will exert themselves more freely, and with less difficulty, if we have before been accustomed to express them in our outward conversations. Nor need we fear the imputation of hypocrisy, though our actions do thus somewhat out-run our affections, seeing they do still proceed from a sense of our duty; and our design is not to appear better than we are, but that we may really become so.

We must endeavour to form internal acts of devotion, charity, etc.

But as inward acts have a more immediate influence on the soul, to mould it to a right temper and frame, so ought we to be most frequent and sedulous in the exercise of them. Let us be often lifting up our hearts toward God; and if we do not say that we love him above all things, let us, at least, acknowledge that it is our duty, and would be our happiness, so to do: let us lament the dishonour done unto him by foolish and sinful men, and applaud the praises and adorations that are given him by that blessed and glorious company above: let us resign and yield ourselves up unto him a thousand times, to be governed by his laws, and disposed of at his pleasure: and, though our stubborn hearts should start back and refuse, yet let us tell him, we are convinced that his will is always just and good; and therefore desire him to do with us whatsoever he pleaseth, whether we will or not.

And so, for begetting in us a universal charity toward men, we must be frequently putting up wishes for their happiness, and blessing every person that we see; and when we have done any thing for the relief of the miserable, we may second it with earnest desires that God would take care of them, and deliver them out of all their distresses.

Thus should we exercise ourselves unto godliness, and when we are employing the powers that we have, the Spirit of God is wont to strike in, and elevate these acts of our soul beyond the pitch of nature, and give them a divine impression; and, after the frequent reiteration of these, we shall find ourselves more inclined unto them, they flowing with greater freedom and ease.

Consideration a great instrument of religion

I shall mention but two other means for begetting that holy and divine temper of spirit which is the subject of the present discourse. And the first is a deep and serious consideration of the truths of our religion, and that both as to the certainty and importance of them. The assent which is ordinarily given to divine truth is very faint and languid, very weak and ineffectual, flowing only from a blind inclination to follow that religion which is in fashion, or a lazy indifference and unconcernedness whether things be so or not.

Men are unwilling to quarrel with the religion of their country, and since all their neighbours are Christians, they are content to be so too; but they are seldom at the pains to consider the evidences of those truths, or to ponder the importance and tendency of them; and thence it is that they have so little influence on their affections and practice.

Those 'spiritless and paralytic thoughts', as one doth rightly term them, are not able to move the will, and direct the hand. We must therefore endeavour to work up our minds to a serious belief and full persuasion of divine truths, unto a sense and feeling of spiritual things: our thoughts must dwell upon them, till we be both convinced of them, and deeply affected with them. Let us urge forward our spirits, and make them approach the invisible world, and fix our minds upon immaterial things, till we clearly perceive that these are no dreams; nay, that all things are dreams and shadows besides them.

When we look about us, and behold the beauty and magnificence of this goodly frame, the order and harmony of the whole creation, let our thoughts from thence take their flight toward that omnipotent wisdom and goodness which did at first produce, and doth still establish and uphold the same.

When we reflect upon ourselves, let us consider that we are not a mere piece of organised matter, a curious and well-contrived engine, that there is more in us than flesh, and blood, and bones - even a divine spark, capable to know, and love, and enjoy our Maker; and though it be now exceedingly clogged with its dull and lumpish companion; yet, ere long, it shall be delivered, and can subsist without the body, as well as that can do without the clothes, which we throw off at our pleasure.

Let us often withdraw our thoughts from this earth, this scene of misery, and folly, and sin, and raise them toward that more vast and glorious world, whose innocent and blessed inhabitants solace themselves eternally in the divine presence, and know no other passion but an unmixed joy, and an unbounded love.

And then consider how the blessed Son of God came down to this lower world to live among us, and die for us, that he might bring us to a portion of the same felicity; and think how he hath overcome the sharpness of death, and opened the kingdom of heaven to all believers, and is now set down on the 'right hand of the Majesty on high' (Hebrews 1:3), and yet is not the less mindful of us, but receiveth our prayers, and presenteth them unto his Father, and is daily visiting his Church with the influences of his Spirit, as the sun reacheth us with his beams.

To beget divine love, we must consider the excellency of the divine nature

The serious and frequent considerations of these, and such other divine truths, is the most proper method to beget that lively faith which is the foundation of religion, the spring and root of the divine life.

Let me further suggest some particular subjects of meditation for producing the several branches of it. And first, to inflame our souls with the love of God, let us consider the excellency of his nature, and his loving-kindness toward us. It is little we know of the divine perfections; and yet that little may suffice to fill our souls with admiration and love, to captivate our affections, as well as to raise our wonder: for we are not merely creatures of sense, that we should be incapable of any other affection but that which entereth by the eyes.

The character of any excellent person whom we have never seen will many times engage our hearts, and make us greatly concerned in all his interests: and what is it, I pray you, that engages us so much to those with whom we converse? I cannot think that it is merely the colour of their face, or their comely proportions, for then we should fall in love with statues, and pictures, and flowers: these outward accomplishments may a little delight the eye, but would never be able to prevail so much on the heart, if they did not represent some vital perfection. We either see or apprehend some greatness of mind, or vigour of spirit, or sweetness of disposition; some sprightliness, or wisdom, or goodness, which charm our spirit, and command our love. Now these perfections are not obvious to the sight, the eyes can only discern the signs and effects of them; and if it be the understanding that directs the affection, and vital perfections prevail with it, certainly the excellencies of the divine nature, the traces whereof we cannot but discover in every thing we behold, would not fail to engage our hearts, if we did seriously view and regard them.

Shall we not be infinitely more transported with that almighty wisdom and goodness which fills the universe, and displays itself in all the parts of the creation, which establisheth the frame of nature, and turneth the mighty wheels of providence, and keepeth the world from disorder and ruin, than with the faint rays of the very same perfections which we meet with in our fellow creatures?

Shall we doat on the scattered pieces of a rude and imperfect picture, and never be affected with the original beauty? This were an unaccountable stupidity and blindness. Whatever we find lovely in a friend, or in a saint, ought not to engross, but to elevate our affection: we should conclude with ourselves, that if there be so much sweetness in a drop, there must be infinitely more in the fountain; if there be so much splendour in a ray, what must the sun be in its glory!

Nor can we pretend the remoteness of the object, as if God were at too great a distance for our converse or our love. 'He is not far from every one of us; for in him we live, and move, and have our being' (Acts 17:27, 28); we cannot open our eyes, but we must behold some footsteps of his glory; and we cannot turn them toward him, but we shall be sure to find his intent upon us, waiting as it were to catch a look, ready to entertain the most intimate fellowship and communion with us.

Let us therefore endeavour to raise our minds to the clearest conceptions of the divine nature; let us consider all that his works do declare, or his Word doth discover of him unto us; and let us especially contemplate that visible representation of him which was made in our own nature by his Son, who was 'the brightness of his glory, and the express image of his person' (Hebrews 1:3), and who appeared in the world to discover at once what God is, and what we ought to be.

Let us represent him unto our minds as we find him described in the gospel; and there we shall behold the perfections of the divine nature, though covered with the veil of human infirmities; and when we have framed unto ourselves the clearest notion that we can of a being, infinite in power, in wisdom, and goodness, the author and fountain of all perfection, let us fix the eyes of our soul upon it (Lamentations 3:58), that our eyes may affect our heart; and, while we are musing, the fire will burn (Psalm 39:3).

We should meditate on his goodness and love
Especially, if hereunto we add the consideration of God's favour and goodwill toward us. Nothing is more powerful to engage our affection to find

that we are beloved. Expressions of kindness
are always pleasing and acceptable unto us,
though the person should be otherwise mean
and contemptible: but, to have the love of one
who is altogether lovely, to know that the glorious Majesty of heaven hath any regard unto us,
how must it astonish and delight us, how must
it overcome our spirits, and melt our hearts,
and put our whole soul into a flame!

Now, as the Word of God is full of the expressions of his love toward man, so all his works do
loudly proclaim it: he gave us our being, and,
by preserving us in it, doth renew the donation
every moment. He hath placed us in a rich and
well-furnished world, and liberally provided for
all our necessities; he raineth down blessings
from heaven upon us, and causeth the earth to
bring forth our provision; he giveth us our food
and raiment, and while we are spending the
productions of one year, he is preparing for us
against another. He sweeteneth our lives with
innumerable comforts, and gratifieth every
faculty with suitable objects: the eye of his
providence is always upon us, and he watcheth
for our safety when we are fast asleep, neither
minding him nor ourselves.

But, lest we should think these testimonies
of his kindness less considerable, because they
are the easy issues of his omnipotent power,
and do not put him to any trouble or pain, he
hath taken a more wonderful method to endear

himself to us; he hath testified his affection to us by suffering as well as by doing; and because he could not suffer in his own nature, he assumed ours. The eternal Son of God did clothe himself with the infirmities of our flesh, and left the company of those innocent and blessed spirits, who knew well how to love and adore him, that he might dwell among men, and wrestle with the obstinacy of that rebellious race to reduce them to their allegiance and felicity, and then to offer himself up as a sacrifice and propitiation for them.

I remember one of the poets hath an ingenious fancy to express the passion wherewith he found himself overcome after a long resistance; that the God of love had shot all his golden arrows at him, but could never pierce his heart, till at length he put himself into the bow, and darted himself straight into his breast. Methinks, this doth some way adumbrate God's method of dealing with men: he had long contended with a stubborn world, and thrown down many a blessing upon them, and when all his other gifts could not prevail, he at last made a gift of himself, to testify his affection, and engage theirs.

The account which we have of our Saviour's life in the gospel, doth all along present us with the story of his love; all the pains that he took, and the troubles that he endured, were the wonderful effects, and uncontrollable evidences of it. But oh! that last, that dismal scene! Is it possible to remember it and question his kindness, or deny him ours? Here, here it is, my dear friend, that we should fix our most serious and solemn thoughts, 'that Christ may dwell in our hearts by faith, that we being rooted and grounded in love, may be able to comprehend with all saints, what is the breadth, and length, and depth, and height: and to know the love of Christ which passeth knowledge, that we may be filled with all the fullness of God' (Ephesians 3:17-19).

We ought also frequently to reflect on those particular tokens of favour and love which God hath bestowed on ourselves; how long he hath borne with our follies and sins, and waited to be gracious unto us, wrestling, as it were, with the stubbornness of our hearts, and essaying every method to reclaim us.

We should keep a register in our minds of all the eminent blessings and deliverances we have met with, some whereof have been so conveyed, that we might clearly perceive they were not the issues of chance, but the gracious effects of the divine favour, and the signal returns of our prayers. Nor ought we to embitter the thoughts of these things with any harsh or unworthy suspicion, as if they were designed on purpose to enhance our guilt, and heighten our eternal damnation. No, no, my friend, God is love, and he hath no pleasure in the ruin of his creatures; if they abuse his goodness, and turn his grace into wantonness, and thereby plunge themselves into the greater depth of guilt and misery, this is the effect of their obstinate wickedness, and not the design of those benefits which he bestows.

If these considerations had once begotten in our hearts a real love and affection towards Almighty God, that would easily lead us unto the other branches of religion; and therefore I shall need say the less of them.

To beget charity, we must remember that all men are nearly related unto God

We shall find our hearts enlarged in charity toward men by considering the relation wherein they stand unto God, and the impresses of his image which are stamped upon them. They are not only his creatures, the workmanship of his hands, but such of whom he taketh special care, and for whom he hath a very dear and tender regard, having laid the designs of their happiness before the foundations of the world, and being willing to live and converse with them to all the ages of eternity. The meanest and most contemptible person whom we behold is the offspring of heaven, one of the children of the Most High; and however unworthy he might behave himself of that relation, so long as God hath not abdicated and disowned him by a final sentence, he will have us to embrace him with a sincere and cordial affection.

You know what a great concernment we are wont to have for those that do anywise belong to the person whom we love; how gladly we lay hold on every opportunity to gratify the child or servant of a friend; and sure, our love toward God would as naturally spring forth in charity toward men, did we mind the interest that he is pleased to take in them, and consider that every soul is dearer unto him than all the material world; and that he did not account the blood of his Son too great a price for their redemption.

That they carry his image upon them

Again, as all men stand in a near relation to God, so they have still so much of his image stamped on them as may oblige and excite us to love them; in some this image is more eminent and conspicuous, and we can discern the lovely tracks of wisdom and goodness; and though, in others, it be miserably sullied and defaced, yet is it not altogether razed, some lineaments at least do still remain.

All men are endued with rational and immortal souls, with understandings and wills capable of the highest and most excellent things; and if they be at present disordered, and put out of tune by wickedness and folly, this may indeed move our compassion, but ought not, in reason, to extinguish our love.

When we see a person of a rugged humour, and perverse disposition, full of malice and dissimulation, very foolish and very proud, it is hard to fall in love with an object that presents itself unto us under an idea so little grateful and lovely. But when we shall consider these evil qualities as the diseases and distempers of a soul which, in itself, is capable of all that wisdom and goodness wherewith the best of saints have ever been adorned, and which may, one day, come to be raised unto such heights of perfection as shall render it a fit companion for the holy angels, this will turn our aversion into pity, and make us behold him with such resentments as we should have when we look upon a beautiful body that was mangled with wounds, or disfigured by some loathsome disease; and however we hate the vices, we shall not cease to love the man.

To beget purity, we should consider the dignity of our nature
In the next place, for purifying our souls, and disentangling our affections from the pleasures and enjoyments of this lower life, let us frequently ponder the excellency and dignity of our nature, and what a shameful and unworthy thing it is for so noble and divine a creature as the soul of man to be sunk and immersed in brutish and sensual lust, or amused with airy and fantastical delights, and so to lose the relish of solid and spiritual pleasures; that the beast should be fed and pampered, and the man and the Christian be starved in us.

Did we but mind who we are, and for what we were made, this would teach us, in a right sense, to reverence and stand in awe of ourselves, it would beget a holy modesty and shamefacedness, and make us very shy and reserved in the use of the most innocent and allowable pleasures.

We should meditate oft on the joys of heaven

It will be very effectual to the same purpose, that we frequently raise our minds toward heaven, and represent to our thoughts the joys that are at God's right hand, 'those pleasures that endure for evermore'; 'for every man that hath this hope in him, purifieth himself, even as he is pure' (1 John 3:3).

If our heavenly country be much in our thoughts, it will make us as 'strangers and pilgrims, to abstain from fleshly lusts, which war against the soul', and keep ourselves 'unspotted from this world', that we may be fit for the enjoyments and felicities of the other.

But then we must see that our notions of heaven be not gross and carnal, that we dream not of a Mohammedan paradise, nor rest on those metaphors and similitudes by which these joys are sometimes represented; for this might perhaps have a quite contrary effect; it might entangle us further in carnal affections, and we should be ready to indulge ourselves in a very liberal foretaste of those pleasures wherein we had placed our everlasting felicity.

But when we come once to conceive aright of those pure and spiritual pleasures, when the happiness we propose to ourselves is from the sight, and love, and enjoyment of God, and our minds are filled with the hopes and forethoughts of that blessed estate, oh! how mean and contemptible will all things here below appear in our eyes! With what disdain shall we reject the gross and muddy pleasures that would deprive us of those celestial enjoyments, or any way unfit and indispose us for them!

Humility arises from the consideration of our failings

The last branch of religion is humility, and sure we can never want matter of consideration for begetting it: all our wickednesses and imperfections, all our follies and our sins, may help to pull down that fond and over-weening conceit which we are apt to entertain of ourselves.

That which makes any body esteem us, is their knowledge or apprehension of some little good, and their ignorance of a great deal of evil that may be in us; were they thoroughly acquainted with us, they would quickly change their opinion.

The thoughts that pass in our heart in the best and most serious day of our life, being exposed unto public view, would render us either hateful or ridiculous; and now, however we conceal our failings from one another; yet sure we are conscious of them ourselves, and some serious reflections upon them would much qualify and allay the vanity of our spirits. Thus holy men have come really to think worse of themselves than of any other person in the world: not but that they knew that gross and scandalous vices are in their nature more heinous than the surprisals of temptations and infirmity, but because they are much more intent on their own miscarriages, than on those of their neighbours, and did consider all the aggravations of the one, and every thing that might be supposed to diminish and alleviate the other.

Thoughts of God give us the lowest thoughts of ourselves
But it is well observed by a pious writer, that the deepest and most pure humility doth not so much arise from the consideration of our own faults and defects, as from a calm and quiet contemplation of the divine purity and goodness. Our spots never appear so clearly as when we place them before this infinite Light; and we never seem less in our own eyes than when we look down upon ourselves from on high. Oh! how little, how nothing do all those shadows of perfection then appear, for which we are wont to value ourselves! That humility which cometh from a view of our own sinfulness and misery, is more turbulent and boisterous, but the other layeth us full as low, and wanteth nothing but that anguish and vexation wherewith our souls are apt to boil when they are the nearest object of our thoughts.

Prayer another instrument of religion. The advantages of mental prayer

There remains yet another means for begetting a holy and religious disposition in the soul; and that is, fervent and hearty prayer.

Holiness is the gift of God, indeed the greatest gift he doth bestow, or we are capable to receive; and he hath promised his Holy Spirit to those that ask it of him. In prayer we make the nearest approaches to God, and lie open to the influences of heaven. Then it is that the sun of righteousness doth visit us with his directest rays, and dissipateth our darkness, and imprinteth his image on our souls.

I cannot now insist on the advantages of this exercise, or the dispositions wherewith it ought to be performed; and there is no need I should, there being so many books that treat on this subject: I shall only tell you, that as there is one sort of prayer wherein we make use of the voice, which is necessary in public, and may sometimes have its own advantages in private, and another wherein, though we utter no sound, yet we conceive the expressions and form the words, as it were, in our minds; so there is a third and more sublime kind of a prayer, wherein the soul takes a higher flight, and having collected all its forces by long and serious meditation, it darteth itself, if I may so speak, toward God in sighs and groans, and thoughts too big for expression.

As when, after a deep contemplation of the divine perfections appearing in all his works of wonder, it addresseth itself unto him in the profoundest adoration of his majesty and glory: or when, after sad reflections on its vileness and miscarriages, it prostrates itself before him with the greatest confusion and sorrow, not daring to lift up its eyes, or utter one word in his presence: or when, having well considered the beauty of holiness, and the unspeakable felicity of those that are truly good, it panteth after God, and sendeth up such vigorous and ardent desires as no words can sufficiently express, continuing and repeating each of these acts as long as it finds itself upheld by the force and impulse of the previous meditation.

This mental prayer is of all others the most effectual to purify the soul, and dispose it unto a holy and religious temper, and may be termed the great secret of devotion, and one of the most powerful instruments of the divine life; and it may be the apostle hath a peculiar respect unto it, when he saith, that 'the Spirit helpeth our infirmities, making intercession for us, with groanings that cannot be uttered'; or, the original may bear, 'that cannot be worded'.

Yet I do not so recommend this sort of prayer as to supersede the use of the other; for we have so many several things to pray for, and every petition of this nature requireth so much time, and so great an intention of spirit, that it were not easy therein to overtake them all - to say nothing, that the deep sighs and heavings of the heart, which are wont to accompany it, are something oppressive to nature, and make it hard to continue long in them. But, certainly, a few of these inward aspirations will do more than a great many fluent and melting expressions.

Religion is to be advanced by the same means by which it is begun, the use of the holy sacrament

Thus, my dear friend, I have briefly proposed the method which I judge proper for moulding the soul into a holy frame; and the same means which serve to beget this divine temper must still be practised for strengthening and advancing it; and therefore I shall recommend but one more for that purpose, and it is the frequent and conscientious use of that holy sacrament which is peculiarly appointed to nourish and increase the spiritual life, when once it is begotten in the soul.

All the instruments of religion do meet together in this ordinance; and while we address ourselves unto it, we are put to practise all the rules which were mentioned before. Then it is that we make the severest survey of our actions, and lay the strictest obligations on ourselves; then are our minds raised to the highest contempt of the world, and every grace doth exercise itself with the greatest activity and vigour; all the subjects of contemplation do there present themselves unto us with the greatest advantage; and then, if ever, doth the soul make its most powerful sallies toward heaven, and assault it with a holy and acceptable force. And certainly the neglect or careless performance of this duty is one of the chief causes that bedwarfs our religion, and makes us continue of so low a size.

But it is time I should put a close to this letter, which is grown to a far greater bulk than at first I intended. If these poor papers can do you the smallest service, I shall think myself very happy in this undertaking; at least I am hopeful you will kindly accept the sincere endeavours of a person who would fain acquit himself of some part of that which he owes you.

A Prayer

And now, O most gracious God, father and fountain of mercy and goodness, who hast blessed us with the knowledge of our happiness, and the way that leadeth unto it, excite in our souls such ardent desires after the one, as may put us forth to the diligent prosecution of the other. Let us neither presume on our own strength, nor distrust thy divine assistance; but while we are doing our utmost endeavours, teach us still to depend on thee for success.

Open our eyes, O God, and teach us out of thy law. Bless us with an exact and tender sense of our duty, and a knowledge to discern perverse things. Oh! that our ways were directed to keep thy statutes, then shall we not be ashamed when we have respect unto all thy commandments.

Possess our hearts with a generous and holy disdain of all those poor enjoyments which this world holdeth out to allure us, that they may never be able to inveigle our affections, or betray us to any sin; turn away our eyes from beholding vanity, and quicken thou us in thy law.

Fill our souls with such a deep sense, and full persuasion of those great truths which thou hast revealed in the gospel, as may influence and regulate our whole conversation, and that the life which we henceforth live in the flesh, we may live through faith in the Son of God.

Oh! that the infinite perfections of thy blessed nature, and the astonishing expressions of thy goodness and love, may conquer and overpower our hearts, that they may be constantly rising toward thee in flames of devoutest affection, and enlarging themselves in sincere and cordial love toward all the world for thy sake: and that we may cleanse ourselves from all filthiness of flesh and spirit, perfecting holiness in thy fear, without which we can never hope to behold and enjoy thee.

Finally, O God, grant that the consideration of what thou art, and what we ourselves are, may both humble and lay us low before thee, and also stir up in us the strongest and most ardent aspirations toward thee. We desire to resign and give up ourselves to the conduct of thy Holy Spirit; lead us in thy truth, and teach us, for thou art the God of our salvation; guide us with thy counsel, and afterward receive us unto glory, for the merits and intercession of thy blessed Son our Saviour. Amen.

Rules and Instructions for a Holy Life

~~~~~~

by
Robert Leighton
Archbishop of Glasgow

For disposing you the better to observe these rules, and profit by them, be pleased to take the following advices.

1. Put all your trust in the special and singular mercy of God, that he, for his mercy's sake and of his holy goodness, will help and bring you to perfection; not that absolute perfection is attainable here, but the meaning is, to high degrees of that spiritual and divine life, which is always growing, and tending toward the absolute perfection above - but in some persons comes nearer to that, and riseth higher, even here, than in the most. If you, with hearty and fervent desires, do continually wish and long for it, and with most humble devotion, daily pray unto God, and call for it, and with all diligence do busily labour and travel to come to it, undoubtedly it shall be given you; for you must not think it sufficient to use exercises, as though they had such virtues in them, that of themselves alone they could make such as do use them perfect; for neither those, nor any other, whatever they be, can of themselves, by their use only, bring
140

unto perfection. But our merciful Lord God, of his own goodness, when you seek with hearty desires and fervent sighings, maketh you to find it when you ask daily with devout prayer, then he giveth it to you; and when you continually, with unwearied labour and travel, knock perseveringly, then he doth mercifully open unto you; and because that those exercises do teach you to seek, ask, and knock, yea, they are none other but very devout petitions, seekings, and spiritual pulsations for the merciful help of God; therefore they are very profitable means to come to perfection by God's grace.

2. Let no particular exercise hinder your public and standing duties to God and your neighbours, but for these rather intermit the other for a time, and then return to them as soon as you can.

3. If in time of your spiritual exercise you find yourself drawn to any better, or to as good a contemplation as that is, follow the track of that good motion so long as it shall last.

4. Always take care to follow such exercises of devout thoughts, withal putting in practice such lessons as they contain and excite to.

5. Though at first ye feel no sweetness in such exercises, yet be not discouraged, nor induced to leave them, but continue them faithfully, whatsoever pain or spiritual trouble ye feel; for doing them for God and his honour, and finding none other present fruit, yet you shall have an

excellent reward for your diligent labour and your pure intentions.

And let not your falling short of these models and rules, nor your daily manifold imperfections and faults, dishearten you; but continue steadfast in your desires, purposes, and endeavours, and ever ask the best, aim at the best, and hope the best, being sorry that you can do no better, and they shall be a most acceptable sacrifice in the sight of God, 'and in due time you shall reap, if you faint not': and of all such instructions, let your rule be to follow them as much as you can; but not too scrupulously thinking your labour lost if you do not exactly and strictly answer them in everything; purpose still better, and, by God's grace, all shall be well.

Section I

Rule 1. Exercise thyself in the knowledge and deep consideration of our Lord God, calling humbly to mind how excellent and incomprehensible he is; and this knowledge shalt thou rather endeavour to obtain by fervent desire and devout prayer than with high study and outward labour; it is the singular gift of God, and certainly very precious. Pray then,

2. 'Most gracious Lord, whom to know is the very bliss and felicity of man's soul, and yet none can know thee, unless thou wilt open and show thyself unto him, vouchsafe of thy infinite mercy now and ever to enlighten my heart and mind to

know thee, and thy most holy and perfect will, to the honour and glory of thy name. Amen.'

3. Then lift up thy heart to consider, not with too great violence, but sobriety, the eternal and infinite power of God, who created all things by his excellent wisdom - his unmeasurable goodness, and incomprehensible love; for he is very and only God, most excellent, most high, most glorious, the everlasting and unchangeable goodness, and eternal substance, a charity infinite, so excellent and ineffable in himself, that all dignity, perfection, and goodness that is possible to be spoke or thought of, cannot sufficiently express the smallest part thereof.

4. Consider that he is the natural place, the centre, and rest of thy soul: if thou then think of the most blessed Trinity, muse not too much thereon, but, with devout and obedient faith, meekly and lowly adore and worship.

5. Consider Jesus the redeemer and husband of thy soul, and walk with him as becomes a chaste spouse, with reverence and lowly shamefulness, obedience and submission.

6. Then turn to the deep, profound consideration of thyself, thine own nothingness, and thy extreme defilement and pollution, thy natural aversion from God, and that thou must by conversion to him again, and union with him, be made happy.

7. Consider thyself and all creatures as nothing, in comparison of thy Lord: that so thou

mayst not only be content, but desirous to be unknown, or, being known, to be contemned and despised of all men, yet without thy faults or deservings, as much as thou canst.

8. 'O God, infuse into my heart thy heavenly light and blessed charity, that I may know and love thee above all things; and above all things loathe and abhor myself. Grant that I may be so ravished in the wonder and love of thee, that I may forget myself and all things, feel neither prosperity nor adversity, may not fear to suffer all the pains of this world, rather than to be parted and pulled away from thee, whose perfections infinitely exceed all thought and understanding. Oh! let me find thee more inwardly and verily present with me than I am with myself, and make me most circumspect how I do use myself in the presence of thee, my holy Lord.

'Cause me always to remember how everlasting and constant is the love thou bearest toward me, and such a charity and continual care as though thou hadst "no more creatures in heaven or earth besides me. What am I? A vile worm and filth".'

9. Then aspire to a great contrition for thy sins, and hatred of them; and abhorring of thyself for them, then crave pardon in the blood of Jesus Christ, and then offer up thyself, soul and body, an oblation or sacrifice in and through him - as they did of old, laying wood on the altar, and

then burning up all; so this shall be a sacrifice of sweet savour, and very acceptable to God.

10. Offer all that thou hast, to be nothing, to use nothing of all that thou hast about thee, and is called thine, but to his honour and glory: and resolve, through his grace, to use all the powers of thy soul, and every member of thy body, to his service, as formerly thou hast done to sin.

11. Consider the passion of thy Lord; how he was buffeted, scourged, reviled, stretched with nails on the cross, and hung on it three long hours, suffered all the contempt and shame, and all the inconceivable pain of it, for thy sake.

12. Then turn thy heart to him, humbly saying, 'Lord Jesus, whereas I daily fall, and am ready to sin, vouchsafe me grace as oft as I shall, to rise again; let me never presume, but always most meekly and humbly acknowledge my wretchedness and frailty, and repent, with a firm purpose to amend; and let me not despair because of my great frailty, but ever trust in thy most loving mercy, and readiness to forgive.'

Section II

1. Thou shalt have much to do in mortifying of thy five senses, which must be all shut up in the crucified humility of Jesus Christ, and be as they were plainly dead.

2. Thou must now learn to have a continual eye inwardly to thy soul, and spiritual life, as thou hast used heretofore to have all thy mind

and regard to outward pleasure and worldly things.

3. Thou must submit and give thyself up unto the discipline of Jesus, and become his scholar, resigning and compelling thyself altogether to obey him in all things: so that thy willing and nilling thou utterly and perfectly do cast away from thee, and do nothing without his licence at every word thou wilt speak, at every morsel thou wilt eat, at every stirring or moving of every article or member of thy body, thou must ask leave of him in thy heart, and ask thyself whether, having so done, that be according to his will and holy example, and with sincere intention of his glory, hence,

4. Even the most necessary actions of thy life, though lawful, yet must thus be offered up with a true intention unto God, in the union of the most holy works and blessed merits of Christ, saying: 'Lord Jesus, bind up in the merits of thy blessed senses all my feeling and sensation, and all my wits and senses, that I never hereafter use them to any sensuality!'

5. Thus labour to come to this union and knitting up of thy senses in God and thy Lord Jesus, and remain so fast to the cross that thou never part from it, and still behave thy body and all thy senses as in the presence of thy Lord God, and commit all things to the most trusty providence of thy loving Lord, who will then order all things delectably and sweetly for thee; reckon all

things besides for right naught, and thus mayst thou come unto wonderful illuminations, and spiritual influence from the Lord thy God.

6. If for his love, thou canst crucify, renounce, and forsake perfectly thyself, and all things; thou must so crucify thyself to all things, and love and desire God only, with thy care and whole heart, that in this most steadfast and strong knot and union unto the will of God, if he would create hell in thee here, thou mightest be ready to offer thyself, by his grace, for his eternal honour and glory, to suffer it, and that purely for his will and pleasure.

7. Thou must keep thy memory clean and pure, as it were a wedlock chamber, from all strange thoughts, fancies and imaginations, and it must be trimmed and adorned with holy meditations and virtues of Christ's holy crucified life and passion: that God may continually and ever rest therein.

Prayer

8. 'Lord, instead of knowing thee, I have sought to know wickedness and sin; and whereas my will and desire were created to love thee, I have lost that love, and declined to the creatures; while my memory ought to be filled with thee, I have painted it with the imagery of innumerable fancies, not only of all creatures, but of all sinful wickedness. Oh! blot out these by thy blood, and imprint thine own blessed image

in my soul, blessed Jesus, by that blood that issued out from thy most loving heart when thou hangedst on the cross. So knit my will to thy most holy will, that I may have no other will but thine, and may be most heartily and fully content with whatsoever thou wilt do to me in this world; yea, if thou wilt, so that I hate thee not, nor sin against thee, but retain thy love, make me suffer the greatest pains.'

Section III

Rule 1. Exercise thyself to the perfect abnegation of all things which may let or impede this union; mortify in thee every thing that is God, nor for God, or which he willeth and loveth not; resigning and yielding up to the high pleasure of God, all love and affection for transitory things; desire neither to have nor hold them, nor bestow or give them, but only for the pure love and honour of God: put away superfluous and unnecessary things, and affect not even things necessary.

2. Mortify all affection to, and seeking of thyself, which is so natural to men, in all the good they desire, and in all the good they do, and in all the evil they suffer; yea, by the inordinate love of the gifts and graces of God, instead of himself, they fall into spiritual pride, gluttony and greediness.

3. Mortify all affection to and delectation in meat and drink, and vain thoughts and fancies,

which though they proceed not to consent, yet they defile the soul, and grieve the Holy Ghost, and do great damage to the spiritual life.

4. Imprint on thy heart the image of Jesus crucified, the impressions of his humility, poverty, mildness, and all his holy virtues; let thy thoughts of him turn into affection, and thy knowledge into love; for the love of God doth most purely work in the mortification of nature; the life of the spirit purifying the higher powers of the soul, begets the solitariness and departure from all creatures, and the influence and flowing into God.

5. Solitude, silence, and the strait keeping of the heart, are the foundations and grounds of a spiritual life.

6. Do all thy necessary and outward works without any trouble or carefulness of mind, and bear thy mind amidst all, always inwardly lifted up and elevated to God, following always more the inward exercise of love than the outward acts of virtue.

7. To this can no man come unless he be rid and delivered from all things under God, and be so swallowed up in God that he can contemn and despise himself and all things; for the pure love of God maketh the spirit pure and simple, and so free, that without any pain and labour, it can at all times turn and recollect itself in God.

8. Mortify all bitterness of heart toward thy neighbours, and all vain complacency in thyself,

all vain-glory and desire of esteem, in words and deeds, in gifts and graces. To this thou shalt come by a more clear and perfect knowledge and consideration of thy own vileness; and by knowing God to be the fountain of all grace and goodness.

9. Mortify all affection toward inward, sensible, spiritual delight in grace, and the following devotion with sensible sweetness in the lower faculties or powers of the soul, which are no ways real sanctity and holiness in themselves, but certain gifts of God to help our infirmity.

10. Mortify all curious investigation or search, all speculation and knowledge of unnecessary things, human or divine; for the perfect life of a Christian consisteth not in high knowledge, but profound meekness; in holy simplicity, and in the ardent love of God; wherein we ought to desire to die to all affection to ourselves, and all things below God; yea, to sustain pain and dereliction, that we may be perfectly knit and united to God, and be perfectly swallowed up in him.

11. Mortify all undue scrupulousness of conscience, and trust in the goodness of God; for our doubting and scruples oft times arise from inordinate self-love, and therefore vex us; they do no good, neither work any real amendment in us; they cloud the soul, and darken faith, and cool love, and it is only the stronger beams of these that can dispel them; and the stronger

that faith and divine confidence is in us, and the hotter divine love is, the soul is so much the more excited and enabled to all the parts of holiness, to mortifications of passions and lusts, to more patience in adversity, and to more thankfulness in all estates.

12. Mortify all impatience in all pains and troubles, whether from the hands of God or men, all desire of revenge, all resentment of injuries, and, by the pure love of God, love thy very persecutors as if they were thy dearest friends.

13. Finally, mortify thy own will in all things, with full resignation of thyself to suffer all dereliction outward and inward, all pain, and pressures, and desolations, and that for the pure love of God: for from self-love, and self-will, spring all sin, and all pain.

Prayer

14. 'O Jesus, my Saviour, thy blessed humility! impress it on my heart, make me most sensible of thy infinite dignity, and of my own vileness, that I may hate myself as a thing of naught, and be willing to be despised, and trodden upon by all, as the vilest mire of the streets, that I may still retain these words, '*I am nothing, I have nothing, I can do nothing, and I desire nothing but one.*'

Section IV

1. Never do any thing with propriety and singular affection, being too earnest, or too much given to it; but with continual meekness of heart and mind, lie at the foot of God, and say, 'Lord, I desire nothing, neither in myself nor in any creature, save only to know and execute thy blessed will,' saying always in thy heart, 'Lord, what wouldst thou have me to do? Transform my will into thine, fill full and swallow up, as it were, my affections with thy love, and with an insatiable desire to honour thee, and despise myself.'

2. If thou aspire to attain to the perfect knitting and union with God, know that it requireth a perfect expoliation and denudation, or bare nakedness, and utter forsaking of all sin, yea, of all creatures, and of thyself particularly: even that thy mind and understanding, thy affections and desires, thy memory and fancy, be made bare of all things in the world, and all sensual pleasures in them; so as thou wouldst be content that the bread which thou eatest had no more savour than a stone, and yet, for his honour and glory that created the bread, thou art pleased that it savoureth so well; but yet from the delectation thou feelest in it, turn thy heart to his praises and love that made it.

3. The more perfectly thou livest in the abstraction and departure, and bare nakedness of thy mind from all creatures, the more nakedly

and purely shalt thou have the fruition of the Lord thy God, and shalt live the more heavenly and angelical a life. Therefore,

4. Labour above all things most exactly to forsake all for him; and chiefly to forsake and contemn thyself, purely loving him; and in a manner forgetting thyself and all things for the vehement burning love of him, that thou wilt take no heed what is sweet or bitter, neither wilt thou consider time nor place, nor mark one person from another, for the wonder and love of thy Lord God, and the desire of his blessed will, pleasure and honour in all things; and whatsoever good thou dost, know and think that God doth it, and not thou.

5. Choose always, to the best of thy skill, what is most to God's honour, and most like unto Christ and his example and most profitable to thy neighbour, and most against thy own proper will, and least serviceable to thy own praise and exaltation.

6. If thou continue faithful in this spiritual work and travel, God at length, without doubt, will hear thy knocking, and will deliver thee from all thy spiritual trouble, from all the tumults, noise and encumbrance of cogitations and fancies, and from all earthly affections, which thou canst by no better means put away, than by continual and fervent desire of the love of God.

7. Do not at any time let or hinder his working, by following thine own will; for, behold how much thou dost the more perfectly forsake thine own will, and the love of thyself, and of all worldly things, so much the more deeply and safely shalt thou be knit unto God, and increase in his true and pure love.

Section V

1. If thou still above all things seek that union, thou must transfund and pour thy whole will into the high pleasure of God; and whatsoever befalls thee, thou must be without murmuring and retraction of heart, accepting it most joyfully for his love, whose will and work it is.

2. Let thy great joy and comfort evermore be, to have his pleasure done in thee, though in pains, sickness, persecutions, oppressions, or inward griefs and pressures of heart, coldness or barrenness of mind, darkening of thy will and senses, or any temptations spiritual or bodily. And,

3. Under any of these be always wary thou turn not to sinful delights, nor to sensual and carnal pleasures, nor set thy heart on vain things, seeking comfort thereby, nor in any ways be idle, but always as thou canst, compel and force thyself to some good spiritual exercise or bodily work; and though they be then unsavoury to thee, yet are they not the less, but the more acceptable to God.

4. Take all afflictions as tokens of God's love to thee, and trials of thy love to him, and purposes of kindness to enrich thee, and increase more plentifully in thee his blessed gifts and spiritual graces, if thou persevere faithfully unto the end, nor leaving off the vehement desire of his love, and thy own perfection.

5. Offer up thyself wholly to him, and fix the point of thy love upon his most blessed increated love, and there let thy soul and heart rest and delight, and be, as it were, resolved and melted most happily into the blessed Godhead; and then take that as a token, and be assured by it, that God will grant thy lovely and holy desire; then shalt thou feel, in a manner, no difference betwixt honour and shame, joy and sorrow; but whatsoever thou perceivest to appertain to the honour of thy Lord, be it ever so hard and un-pleasant to thyself, thou wilt heartily embrace it, yea, with all thy might follow and desire it; yet, when thou hast done what is possible for thee, thou wilt think thou hast done nothing at all; yea, thou shalt be ashamed, and detest thyself, that thou hast so wretchedly and imperfectly served so noble and worthy a Lord; and therefore thou wilt desire and endeavour every hour to do and suffer greater and more perfect things than hitherto thou hast done, forgetting the things that are behind, and pressing forward, etc.

6. If thou hast in any measure attained to love and abide in God, then mayst thou keep the

powers of thy soul and thy senses, as it were, shut up in God, from gadding out to any worldly thing or vanity, as much as possible, where they have so joyful a security and safeness: satiate thy soul in him, and in all other things still see his blessed presence.

7. Whatsoever befalleth thee, receive it not from the hand of any creature, but from him alone, and render back all to him, seeking in all things his pleasure and honour - the purifying and subduing thyself. What can harm thee, when all must first touch God, within whom thou hast inclosed thyself?

8. When thou perceivest thyself thus knit to God, and thy soul more fast and joined nearer to him than to thine own body, then shalt thou know his everlasting, and incomprehensible, and ineffable goodness, and the true nobleness of thy soul that came from him, and was made to be reunited to him.

9. If thou wouldst ascend and come up to thy Lord God, thou must climb up by the wounds of his blessed humanity, that remain, as it were, for that use; and when thou art got up there, thou wouldst rather suffer death than willingly commit any sin.

10. Entering into Jesus, thou castest thyself in an infinite sea of goodness, that more easily drowns and happily swallows thee up than the ocean does a drop of water. Then shalt thou be hid and transformed in him, and shalt often

be as thinking without thought, and knowing without knowledge, and loving without love, comprehended of him whom thou canst not comprehend.

Section VI

1. Too much desire to please men mightily pre-judgeth the pleasing of God.

2. Too great earnestness and vehemency, and too greedy delight in bodily work and external doings, scattereth and loseth the tranquillity and calmness of the mind.

3. Cast all thy care on God, and commit all to his good pleasure; laud, and praise, and applaud him in all things small and great; forsake thy own will, and deliver up thyself freely and cheerfully to the will of God, without reserve or exception, in prosperity, in adversity, sweet or sour, to have or to want, to live or to die.

4. Disunite thy heart from all things, and unite it only to God.

5. Remember often, and devoutly, the life and passion, the death and resurrection of our Saviour, Jesus.

6. Descant not on other men's deeds, but consider thine own; forget other men's faults, and remember thine own.

7. Never think highly of thyself, nor despise any other man.

8. Keep silence and retirement as much as thou canst, and through God's grace they will keep thee from snares and offences.

9. Lift up thy heart often to God, and desire in all things his assistance.

10. Let thy heart be filled, and wholly taken up with the love of God, and of thy neighbour, and do all that thou dost in that sincere charity and love.

The Sum is:

1. Remember always the presence of God.
2. Rejoice always in the will of God. And,
3. Direct all to the glory of God.

Section VII

1. Little love, little trust; but a great love brings a great confidence.

2. That is a blessed hope that doth not slacken us in our duty, nor maketh us secure, but increaseth both a cheerful will, and gives greater strength to mortification and all obedience.

3. What needest thou, or why travellest thou about so many things; think upon one, desire and love one and thou shalt find great rest. Therefore,

4. Wherever thou be, let this voice of God be still in thine ear: 'My son, return inwardly to thy heart, abstract thyself from all things, and mind me only.' Thus:

5. With a pure mind in God, clean and bare from the memory of all things, remaining un-moveably in him, thou shalt think and desire nothing but him alone; as though there were nothing else in the world but he and thou only together; that all thy faculties and powers being thus re-collected into God, thou mayst become one spirit with him.

6. Fix thy mind on thy crucified Saviour, and remember continually his great meekness, love, and obedience, his pure chastity, his unspeak-able patience, and all the holy virtues of his humanity.

7. Think on his mighty power and infinite goodness; how he created and redeemed thee, how he justifieth thee, and worketh in thee all virtues, graces, and goodness; and thus remem-ber him, until thy memory turn into love and affection. Therefore,

8. Draw thy mind thus from all creatures, unto a certain silence, and rest from the jangling and company of all things below God; and when thou canst come to this, then is thy heart a place meet and ready for thy Lord God to abide in, there to talk with thy soul.

9. True humility gaineth and overcometh God Almighty, and maketh thee also apt and meet to receive all graces and gifts; but, alas! who can say that he hath this blessed meekness? it being so hard, so uncertain, so secret and unknown a thing to forsake and mortify perfectly and

exactly thyself, and that most venomous worm of all goodness, vain-glory.

10. Commit all to the high providence of God, and suffer nothing to rest or enter into thy heart, save only God: all things in the earth are too base to take up thy love or care, or to trouble thy noble heart, thy immortal and heavenly mind. Let them care and sorrow or rejoice about these things who are of the world, for whom Christ would not pray.

11. Thou canst not please nor serve two masters at once; thou canst not love divers and contrary things; if, then, thou wouldst know what thou lovest, mark well what thou thinkest most upon. Leave earth, and have heaven; leave the world, and have God.

12. All sin and vice springeth from the property of our own will; all virtue and perfection cometh and groweth from the mortifying of it, and the resigning of it wholly to the pleasure and will of God.